DESIGN

FOR

DEMENTIA

DESIGN FOR DEMENTIA

Edited by
Stephen Judd
Mary Marshall
Peter Phippen

Published by
The Journal of Dementia Care
London, England

First published in 1998 by
Journal of Dementia Care
Hawker Publications Ltd
13 Park House
140 Battersea Park Road
London SW11 4NB
Tel: (+44) 171 720 2108
Fax: (+44) 171 498 3023

British Library Cataloguing in Publication Data

A catalogue record for this book is available
from the British Library

ISBN 1-874790-35-3

Design by Jay Dowle
Cover by Sue Lishman

Printed and bound in Great Britain by
BR Hubbard, Dronfield

The Journal of Dementia Care
The Journal of Dementia Care is published six times a year and is recognised as
the leading specialist journal on dementia. For subscription enquiries please contact
Hawker Publications at the address above.

Contents

Block plans

Patrick House
Page 25

Hasselknuten
Page 30

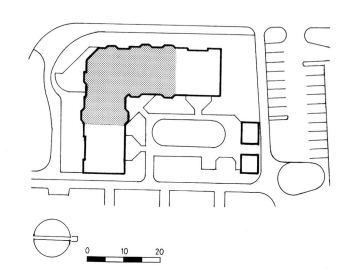

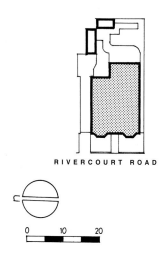

RIVERCOURT ROAD

0   10   20

0   10   20

Carntyne Gardens
Page 37

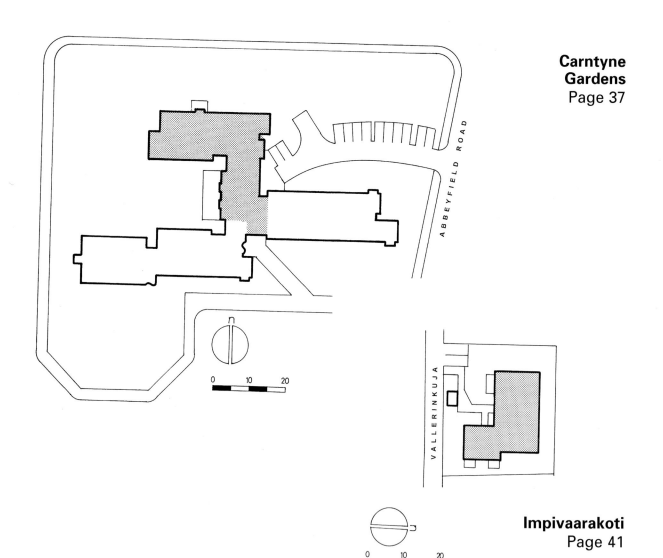

ABBEYFIELD ROAD

VALLERINKUJA

0   10   20

0   10   20

Impivaarakoti
Page 41

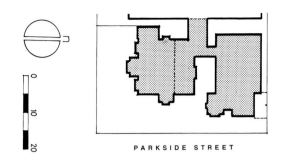

PARKSIDE STREET

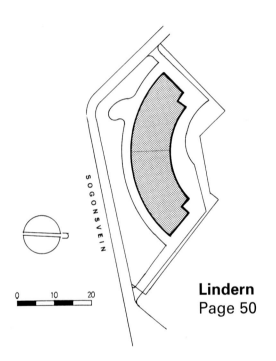

S O G O N S V E I N

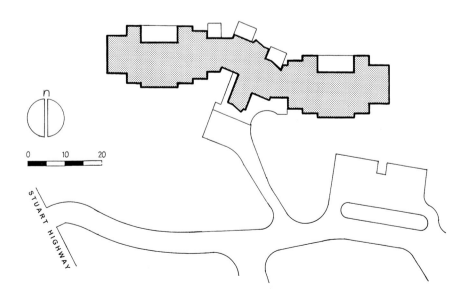

STUART HIGHWAY

Block plans

Annalakoti + Pekkalakoti
Page 73

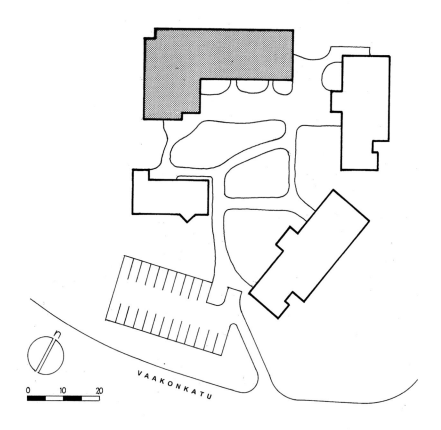

VAAKONKATU

0   10   20

Sidegate Lane
Page 78

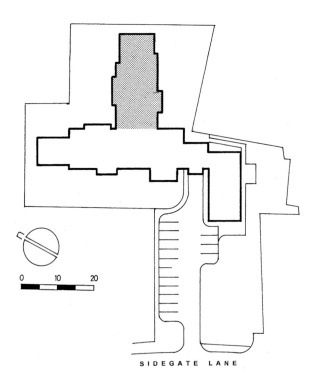

SIDEGATE LANE

0   10   20

Aldersgate Village
Page 91

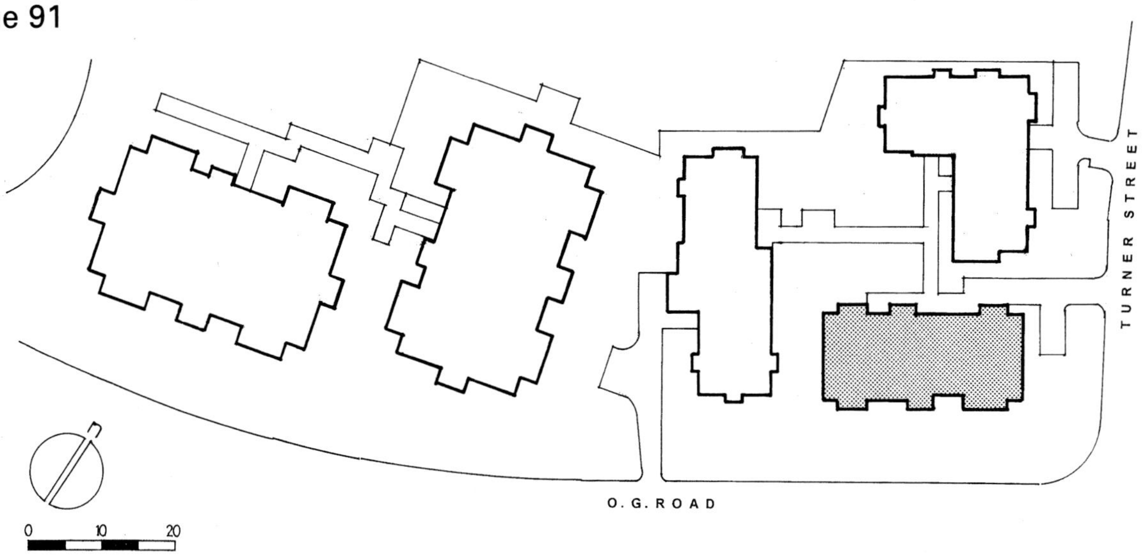

TURNER STREET

O.G. ROAD

0   10   20

ADARDS
Page 98

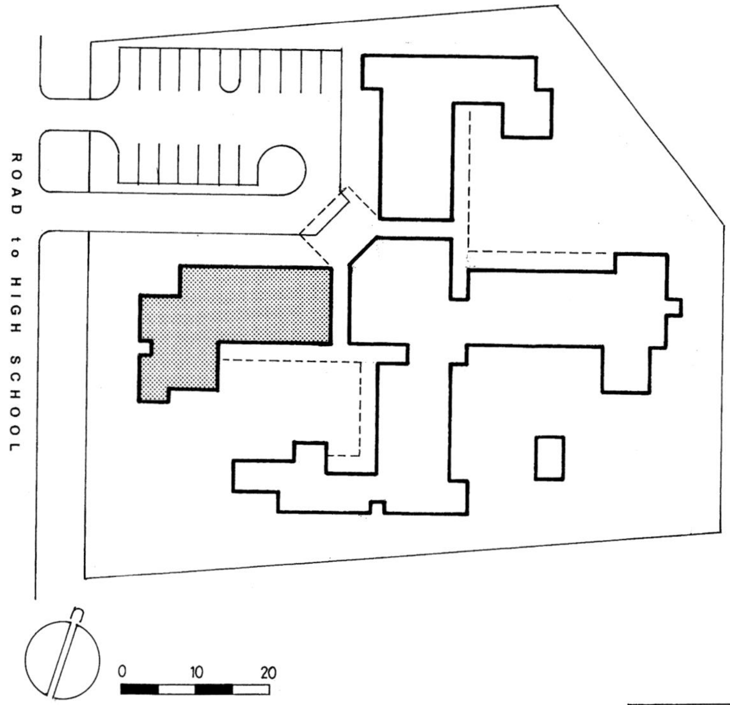

ROAD to HIGH SCHOOL

0   10   20

Woodlands
Page 105

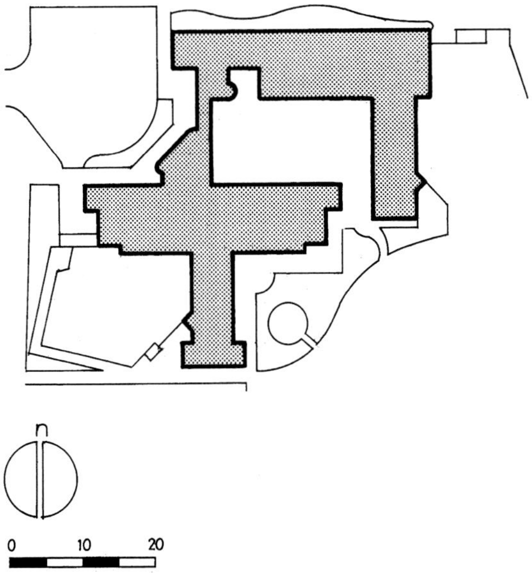

0   10   20

Block plans

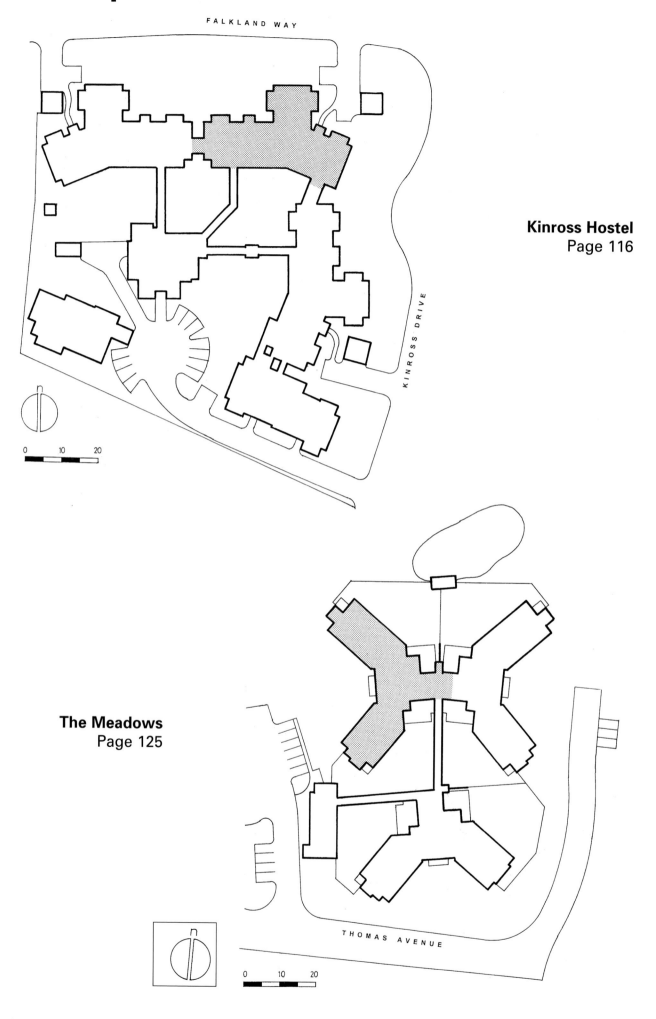

FALKLAND WAY

Kinross Hostel
Page 116

KINROSS DRIVE

0   10   20

The Meadows
Page 125

THOMAS AVENUE

0   10   20

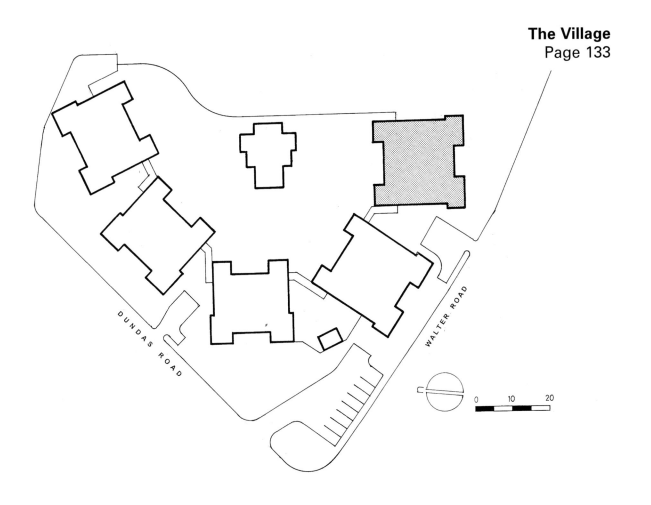

The Village
Page 133

DUNDAS ROAD

WALTER ROAD

0   10   20

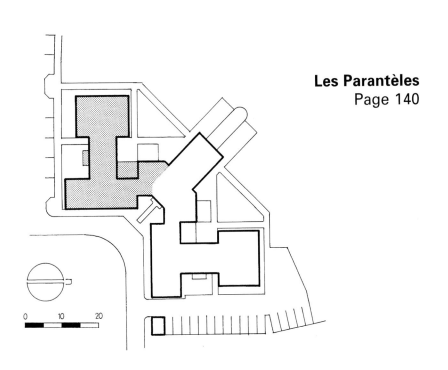

Les Parantèles
Page 140

0   10   20

Design for Dementia

THE TWENTY buildings described in this book were chosen by the editors because they illustrate thoughtful and thoroughgoing attempts to design a therapeutic environment for groups of people with dementia. They illustrate the state of this art in Australia and Northern Europe in the same way that Cohen and Day's book *Contemporary Environments for People with Dementia* does for North America.

The buildings were known to the editors for various reasons and most of them have been visited by more than one of us. They represent certain key characteristics. They tend to be small (no more than 13 residents per unit, although some are in larger clusters) because they aim for a familiar, domestic, orientating character. A list of their shared characteristics would note that they are all: small; domestic; have concealed staff rooms/offices; are accessible, provide safe outside space; their residents are helped to find their way about by exceptional (and sometimes total) visual access; they have dining/sitting rooms; and are generally pleasant, well-designed buildings.

They all try and fit into their localities. As such they do not draw attention to their purpose. This means that they look very different. Several, for example, are more than single-storey because they exist in urban settings. Considerable effort has been made in each case to be both culturally- and age-appropriate; and yet to be capable of accommodating the different tastes of residents in terms of furniture and other belongings.

We do not consider any of them an ideal exemplar. Indeed we might well argue amongst ourselves about the qualities an ideal exemplar would possess. They all, however, have a great many qualities worth replicating. Brief summaries of their special qualities, as we see them, precede each entry. A full summary of all their features is provided in the fold-out matrices.

People with dementia represent a large and increasing group of disabled people in industrialised societies. We hope the entries will provide real examples to assist the many professionals struggling to find design solutions for those who need group living settings.

The editors had the idea for this book and we chose the buildings but it would not have been possible to produce it without the enthusiastic help of the owners and the architects who provided all the details of the buildings featured. We are most grateful to them all. We take full responsibility for any errors which may have crept into the text.

Stephen Judd
Mary Marshall
Peter Phippen

The editors would like to thank Martin Bedwell, Jane Pearson, Carl von Buen (in the UK); Owe Ahlund, Inga-Britt Johansson, Bob Scott, Ursula Ostby, Torhild Holthe, Annikki Korhonen, Päivi Karjalainen (in Scandinavia); Linda Benattar (France); Bella Cammelbeeck (Holland); Leanne Copland, Kirsty Bennett, Brian Kidd, Peter McHale, Penny Flett, Gretta Peachment, Stephen Alexander, Imas Thompson, Sharon Davis, Di Oldfield, Del Heuke and John Tooth (Australia) for their help in collecting information, translation and organising the visits which took place during the writing of this book.

Design for Dementia

The editors

Stephen Judd

Stephen Judd BA, PhD is chief executive of the Hammond Care Group, which is based in Sydney, Australia. Hammond Care provides direct care services for more than 450 people and exists to nurture dignity and improve the quality of life for older people and dementia sufferers, especially those least able to provide for themselves.

Stephen has more than fifteen years experience in the healthcare and information technology industries. Prior to being appointed Chief Executive of Hammond Care, Stephen was the General Manager of the networking division of Techway, a publicly-listed Australian company. Stephen lives in Sydney and is married with three children.

Mary Marshall

Professor Mary Marshall MBE, MA, DSA, DASS is the director of the Dementia Services Development Centre at the University of Stirling, Scotland. She has worked with, and for, older people for most of her career as a social worker, lecturer, researcher and voluntary organisation manager. She has written and edited several books about working with older people.

The Dementia Services Development Centre exists to improve services for people with dementia and their carers and as such it receives many requests for assistance on the design of specialist units.

Peter Phippen

Peter Phippen OBE, Dip Arch (RWA), RIBA was a founding partner of Phippen Randall and Parkes and is a director of PRP Architects.

He has recently concentrated on private sector housing, including high density urban projects and on housing for older people, particularly those with dementia as well as physical frailty. He has recently studied projects for people with dementia in Australia, Europe and Scandinavia.

He is a member of the Urban Design Group and is particularly interested in the design of housing settlements and satisfying the demands of the private and social sectors to secure variety and social cohesion.

He was a member of the working group which reviewed the workings of DB 32 for the Department of the Environment and the Department of Transport. He is a director of the Housing Centre Trust.

Peter was trained at the RWA School of Architecture in Bristol, gained experience with the GLC, taught at the Architectural Association, and was a founding member of a housing association, remaining a committee member for some years. For 30 years he has been responsible in PRP for a wide spectrum of work in both private and public sectors and now acts as chairman and is responsible for business development.

He was awarded the Order of the British Empire in 1977, and has been an assessor for design awards for a number of architectural competitions. He has given papers on housing design at seminars and conferences and lectured at schools of architecture.

Therapeutic buildings for people with dementia

By Mary Marshall

THIS BOOK ARISES from an increased awareness that the built environment can have a fundamental effect on a person with dementia: probably greater than on people who are mentally fit. Taira (1990) points out that the environment has the greatest effect on the person with the least capacity. It is crucially important that the expertise which exists is made easily available to all concerned, in as usable a fashion as possible. The editors intend that, by describing 18 well-designed buildings, readers will see design features in the whole rather than isolated in a design guide.

The focus on Australia and Northern Europe is deliberate. Cohen and Day (1993) have produced a very influential book on similar lines with mainly North American examples. It is timely to make more widely available the expertise of Australia and Northern Europe, both to illustrate what is different and to capitalise on rich and well established pools of expertise.

This book is written for a wide range of professionals responsible for designing such buildings: executives from agencies, service providers commissioning new buildings or adapting older ones; officials from regulatory authorities; staff responsible for inspection and approval of building standards; fire safety and environmental health officers; architects and interior designers, as well as nursing and other related professionals.

Dementia is a set of diseases of the brain which affects mainly, although not entirely, older people, and especially people aged over 80. The largest group develop Alzheimer's disease, followed by Lewy body dementia and vascular dementia. Relatively rare causes include Pick's disease, Creutzfeldt Jacob disease and Korsakoff's disease. These rarer causes generally occur in younger people and raise special design challenges which have not yet been addressed. Korsakoff's disease, for example, is related to excess alcohol consumption and may result from a particular lifestyle.

Another younger group are those whose dementia occurs alongside another illness or disability. People with AIDS sometimes get dementia and have particular needs. A building for this group of people is included in this book. People with Down's syndrome usually get dementia. Their design needs have not yet been addressed in either Northern Europe or Australia although there are at least two buildings in Australia in the planning stage (1998).

There are increasing numbers of people with dementia as the population ages. About one in ten people aged over 60 has dementia and this increases to one in five people over eighty. In most of the more developed countries in the world this is a rapidly growing group of people. Other new groups such as people with Down's syndrome in their forties and fifties are also emerging in more developed countries.

Less developed countries will be facing the challenge of providing for people with dementia within the next twenty years or so as the children who survived infancy for the first time enter old age. The principles of design apply in any country.

In the past people with dementia with needs for care greater than the capacity of their family or friends to provide it, lived in large psychiatric hospitals. These are now being phased out in all the countries where they have been a significant model of care. As a consequence many more people with dementia are being placed in alternative facilities or are remaining at home. Sadly this book does not include examples of ordinary dwellings designed for dementia because they are very rare and we were unable to find any of significant quality.

A disability approach

It is very easy to emphasise the gloomy aspects of this mainly terminal disease because it does have such a devastating impact on the lives of people with dementia and their families and friends. Only recently has a more optimistic approach emerged. This optimism is not related to treatment and medication to any extent since drugs are only efficacious with a minority of people with dementia.

The optimism derives from an increased understanding of the impact the built and social environment has on people with dementia. In the UK the major exponent of this "new culture of dementia care" is Tom Kitwood. (See for example Kitwood and Benson 1995.) Kitwood and others suggest that people with dementia function at very different levels with the same level of neurological damage. Some other factors are therefore clearly at work and these seem to include the personality and background of the person and the impact of both the buildings in which they live and the people relating to them. If the buildings and their carers relate to people with dementia as individuals, reinforce their sense of well-being and provide opportunities for them to practise their remaining skills, then the people with dementia are helped to function at their greatest potential.

As far as design is concerned it is helpful to see dementia as a disability. This approach provides clear pointers to the disabilities for which a building needs to compensate. Dementia as a disability is characterised by:
- impaired memory
- impaired reasoning
- impaired ability to learn
- high level of stress
- acute sensitivity to the social and the built environment.

The broad design implications of this are – or should be – obvious, at the general level. Buildings should not rely on the person having any memory of where they are or how they got there. Buildings should not rely on people remembering where to go. Buildings should minimise stress. This book describes 20 buildings which the editors consider achieve this effectively.

It can be helpful to differentiate between a disease model and a disability model in approaching design for dementia since the majority of current buildings are based on the former. The two models should not be seen as mutually exclusive but rather as having a difference in emphasis. The disease model is exemplified in definitions of dementia such as:

Dementia is a group of progressive diseases of the brain that slowly affect all the functions of the mind and lead to a deterioration in a person's ability to concentrate, remember and reason. It can affect every area of human thinking, feeling and reasoning (Murphy 1986).

This approach to dementia care would tend to focus on the inevitability of decline. Design considerations would be to keep people comfortable, safe and clean, and to provide a building which takes account of behaviour such as wandering. In other words this approach does not prioritise the potential for buildings to assist functioning and prevent behaviour difficulties. This approach is still the one held by the majority of professionals in the field of dementia care, although the disability approach seems to be more widely accepted in Australia. The disease approach still therefore imbues the design briefs written for architects and, since it is the view held by most of the public, it is the one shared by most architects too. It tends to result in large, clinical units. If the potential for therapeutic design is embraced at all by people adopting a disease model, it tends to be only in designing buildings for those in the early stages of dementia.

We do not want to give the impression that we think health services are unaware of the impact of design on people with dementia, nor do we want to say that the non-medical models are better. In our experience some of the most sensitive design features can be in medical and nursing settings, whereas there are some very disabling buildings provided by welfare agencies. However, the buildings in this book do tend to be non-medical in the sense of not being psychiatric service buildings. This is in large part because there was much more choice among specialised nursing homes, hostels, residential homes and care housing units.

International consensus

Design for people with dementia has not been subjected to the scrutiny of research in the same way as medication, for example. Lawton (1987) is the pre-eminent researcher in the field of "person-environment relations". His work confirms that design does have an impact on people using buildings. However the work on the impact of specific aspects of design is very rare. Some research studies have compared small and large units: Lindesay *et al* (1991), Ritchie *et al* (1992), Plaisier *et al* (1992), in terms of the functioning of people with dementia. However, these studies do not separate out design from other aspects of care. Netten (1993) did identify design features in her study of people with dementia in non-specialist units. Smaller sub-units and adequate lighting were identified as helpful. Wilkinson *et al* (1995) looked at toilet door signs and, for people in the earlier stages of dementia, came out in favour of a particular design.

Given a paucity of research, it is significant that there is an almost unanimous consensus about good design for dementia. The major source of published material is the USA: Cohen and Weisman (1991), Cohen and Day (1993), Calkins (1988), Hiatt (1995), Peppard (1991), Shroyer *et al* (1989). In the UK Norman (1987) and Netten (1993) have been influential. Certain buildings have had a major impact, in part because of their energetic proponents. The CADE (Confused and Disturbed Elderly) units of New South Wales, Australia, one of which is included in this book (Fleming and Bowles 1987), and the Corinne Dolan Alzheimer Centre, Heather Hill, Chardon, Ohio are widely quoted as exemplars. It is hoped that this book will extend that repertoire by giving credit to some excellent buildings which have not yet found proponents.

There are two ways of summarising this international consensus. One is agreement on principles, the other agreement on design features.

The consensus on principles of design includes:
- design should compensate for disability
- design should maximise independence
- design should enhance self-esteem and confidence
- design should demonstrate care for staff
- design should be orientating and understandable
- design should reinforce personal identity
- design should welcome relatives and the local community
- design should allow control of stimuli.

The consensus on design features includes:
- small size
- familiar, domestic, homely in style
- plenty of scope for ordinary activities (unit kitchens, washing lines, garden sheds)
- unobtrusive concern for safety
- different rooms for different functions
- age-appropriate furniture and fittings
- safe outside space
- single rooms big enough for lots of personal belongings
- good signage and multiple cues where possible e.g. sight, smell, sound
- use of objects rather than colour for orientation;
- enhancement of visual access
- controlled stimuli, especially noise.

The selection of buildings

The buildings in this book meet these criteria to a notable extent and have an additional ingredient which is that they are pleasing buildings in themselves. In other words, good design for people with dementia has to have the same qualities that any good building has. We are not suggesting in this book that buildings for people with dementia can be built to a formula. Architects need to take the brief to meet the criteria and then create a pleasing place to live.

Unresolved issues

A great range of issues make designing for dementia a challenge even with a high degree of international consensus on the desired outcome. These include:

1. Cost

Cost is the most often quoted reason for not providing

therapeutic design. There are numerous aspects to this. Here we want to mention only a couple. The first is the issue of size. Small scale is at the top of the list of key design features. What this actually means is widely divergent. The gruppebuendes in Sweden house between six and eight people. The Scottish Health Service guidelines have consistently recommended eight or ten. Heather Hill in Ohio has 12 people in each unit. The maximum size of any unit in this book is 14 in the actual living unit (although the overall numbers in any cluster of units may be greater). This is a cost issue, primarily because of the staffing implications. Staff is the major cost (or expense) consideration. The usual aim is to provide the minimum number of staff for a group of people with dementia to achieve good care. Excluding cooks and domestic staff and including activity staff the preferred ratio is usually 1:4-1:7 staff to one person with dementia; although it depends greatly on the needs of the people being cared for. Providing units in multiples of 4-7 is usually seen as the only cost-effective way to proceed. Many units deliberately not included in this book are for 20 people with five staff which is plainly indivisible except into units of six, which are not perceived as practical.

The second cost issue we wish to mention is that of designing for groups with different needs. People with dementia are far from a homogenous group, not least in the extent of their concomitant physical disabilities which, along with behaviour, is the way usually used to differentiate groups. There are design implications for both issues. People with challenging behaviours, for example, may need a great deal more visual access in the sense that they need to be able to see the staff and the staff need to be able to see them. It is clearly cheapest to build a standard building – which is how the larger nursing home companies achieve savings. However, this will not work with dementia care.

2. Regulations

Every country has fire and environmental health regulations which are essential to ensure that people using buildings, which are not their homes, are not put at risk. Fire regulations are usually concerned with ensuring that people can get out of a building or into a fire protected space with all speed. They usually specify the distance between any one safe area and the next, and are particularly concerned with rooms in which fire risks are greatest such as kitchens and boiler rooms.

Environmental health regulations are concerned with the transmission of disease through contaminated surfaces generally related to food preparation and consumption.

There are numerous difficulties with this apparently sensible system of legislation and inspection. The first is the tension which exists about the nature of the buildings in which people with dementia live when they are unable to live at home. They are classed as institutions or public buildings and are therefore subject to stringent regulation. The aim of most of the design principles and features listed above is that the person with dementia is living in a group environment as much like a normal house as possible. The provision of a normal kitchen with normal fittings is, for example, an essential component of such an approach. Yet this is rarely acceptable to fire officers. If they agree at all, it is only with stern requirements for a fireproof room which means that the kitchen is either sealed off and unrecognisable, or the unit is divided by fireproof walls in such a way that concepts of domesticity and orientation are severely compromised. A normal kitchen is often unacceptable to environmental health officers too who require stainless steel and coolers in a kitchen. They often also require the installation of a small additional sink for hand-washing, which is thoroughly confusing for people with dementia.

This seems to be a particularly British problem. In Australia the requirements for a small shared dwelling are less institutional and more flexible: since Aldersgate in 1984 (which is featured in this book) there has been greater recognition that these dwellings are houses, not institutions. In Sweden the principles of domestic design for people with dementia override the usual regulations. Indeed the regulations specify the characteristics of dementia design.

It also seems that British regulations have not kept pace with technological changes such as effective sprinkler systems, smoke alarms and the trend towards providing a safe space, rather than evacuation, when dealing with mentally or physically disabled people.

Another difficulty is the interpretation of the legislation which varies greatly over the UK. Some officers are much more cautious than others. It is an expensive and often delaying business to take issue with each interpretation.

3. Cultural appropriateness

If we genuinely believe that people with dementia retain their past memories longer than their present it behoves us to provide designs which make sense in an era or a style familiar to the residents as younger people. There are several challenges to this: One is that the units have a mixed population in terms of class, ethnic background, occupational history. A homogenous group is always easiest to design for. For example an aboriginal nursing home in Kalgoorlie, Western Australia, can provide a log fire in the middle of the day room and that makes sense for all the residents. A single Aboriginal man in a nursing home in Northam may have to orientate himself to an environment designed for the wheat belt farmers. Many units are intimidatingly posh for some residents. It must help to furnish single rooms with familiar furniture, ideally the resident's own furniture. Yet many rooms are kitted out with fitted furniture or there is no storage to allow the room to be emptied for the resident's own furniture.

Ethnic background is rarely taken seriously in design terms. In Australia many migrants will have spent their early lives in countries such as Greece and Scotland, yet the design of units still tends to reflect early twentieth-century "Federation" Australian design. In the UK the same applies. Rarely are there design concessions to an Asian or Italian background, for example.

4. A home for life?

Whether or not a person with dementia is to remain in one unit until they die is a key issue in determining the design of units. We would all like to think that this is possible since it is certainly, at first glance, desirable. It is rarely good for any of us to move and moving someone with impaired reasoning can be very stressful. Having said that, many people with dementia thrive in a new environment if it better suits their needs. Sadly the general rule of thumb seems to be that the more mentally disabled you are the more disabling the environment provided.

Coons (1991) is not the only expert to stress that homogeneity of need is a determinant of good quality care for people with dementia. As we have said before, people with dementia are far from a homogenous group. At the most basic level people with dementia will vary in terms of their physical disabilities and will make very different demands on the environment in this respect e.g. in terms of incontinence or mobility, or need for terminal care. They will also have very different behaviours. Some people with dementia cope by walking great distances. Others can be extremely anxious and agitated and require to see staff at all times. Dependency scales, such as REPDS (the Revised Elderly Persons Disability Scale), provide a more rounded picture of the kind of dependencies which need to be considered.

The design implications of homogeneity or lack of it are many. A unit where people are physically very disabled may require space for hoists, drips, oxygen, etc. Space for sluices and for the storage of wheelchairs may need to be provided. On the other hand a home for people who have retained many skills and physical abilities, but have severe memory problems, may be more like an ordinary house. (Indeed, it may be an ordinary house. It is likely that over the next five years or so we will see a rapid increase in expertise in adapting or designing ordinary houses so people can remain in their own homes.) People with high levels of agitation and challenging behaviours may need units where there are very high levels of visual access so they can see the staff at all times and the staff can see them. The issue of whether or not high levels of visual access are desirable for all people with dementia is unresolved. Yet it would seem sensible to design for the highest levels of disability in this respect so that people with dementia can increase their chances of remaining *in situ*.

Attitudes to moving people to settings where they are with a more homogeneous group vary. In Australia and Sweden it seems much more acceptable. Units for people with some social competence and relatively low levels of physical dependence are widespread and are designed on the assumption that people will move if they begin to disrupt the lives of others in the unit or need high levels of physical care. In the UK there is a resolute commitment to the rhetoric of a home for life, although moving people does occasionally happen.

Whether or not a principle of moving to a more homogenous group is adopted, attention needs to be paid to the environment of the most disabled.

Building for dementia: a matter of design

By Stephen Judd

BEFORE STARTING to think about building for people with dementia, it is important to stop and ask: "What do we want to achieve?" Do we want to provide housing for people who have a degenerative disease? Do we want to provide the ideal environment for nurses, so that they can deliver the best of clinical care? Do we want to protect people, from themselves and from others?

If these are our primary goals – and they are well-intentioned – the chances are that we would not design anything like the case studies in this book. Because although the case studies come from a variety of cultures, in different locations thousands of kilometres apart, each with their own physical milieu and site-specific challenges, all of them resonate with a philosophy of care which expresses two distinct objectives:

● to promote improvement; and
● to compensate for individual dysfunction.

Each design aims to ensure that the physical environment assists – rather than detracts – from the promotion of those two goals.

How do these buildings achieve this? There appear to be five recurring design themes which ignore the very real cultural and locational differences.

1. The environment should be small
At first glance, this seems an extraordinary statement. Certainly the Swedish and Norwegian examples are clearly small, with between six or eight people living together. But there are other centres with more than forty people on sites of more than 8,000 square metres. How can that be deemed small? On closer analysis, however, virtually all of the designs of these larger case studies have sought to reduce the size of the environment – from the perspective of the individual resident. There are individual houses for eight to fourteen residents and, in turn, there are various designs to reduce the size of these houses even further. Both The Village at Inglewood and Kinross Hostel in Western Australia have five and three houses respectively; the largest centre, Les Parentèles in Chars, France has six houses of ten; Moorside and Sidegate Lane in England have their residents in three different wings; while the "Y" design of the homes at The Meadows reduces homes of twelve and fourteen people into two smaller groups of six and seven.

All of the case studies have an aversion to bigness – both in a spatial and a numerical sense. Bigness is perceived as promoting confusion while smallness assists in enhancing comprehension. In terms of scale, the buildings in their exterior and interior perspectives are small. Most have small domestic, rather than commercial, kitchens. Corridors, if they exist at all, are short and not overly wide. Sometimes effort has been made to shorten them visually with the use of hampers

(e.g. Hasselknuten in Stenungsund and The Meadows in Sydney). The hospital model has been jettisoned in favour of a more domestic scale.

2. The environment should be familiar
All of the case studies sought to provide an environment which was familiar to the resident. This was almost invariably a "homelike" environment, with domestic scale and features rather than institutional ones. There is the desire that the environment be "home" for each resident. This is easily said, but much harder to achieve. One person's sense of home, and how they would describe it, will almost certainly be different from another person's. And yet these environments are seeking to be "home" for all residents.

There have been a number of different approaches to this challenge. Re-modelled buildings often use the features of the older, converted spaces. The "group living" in converted apartments at Stenungsund in Sweden, for example, is typical of what a vast number of Swedes call "home". By contrast, Parkside Court in Melbourne, Australia has used the architectural features of high moulded ceilings, open fireplace surrounds, generous-sized bedrooms and the open, eat-in kitchens of an early twentieth-century house to provide a sense of domesticity with which many older Australians would be familiar.

The newer, purpose-built facilities have incorporated familiar features which have promoted homeliness rather than institutionalism. The Australian pioneer in promoting this homeliness was architect Brian Kidd. The opening in 1984 of stage one of Aldersgate Nursing Home in South Australia signalled a landmark victory against the regulatory paradigm as to what constituted a permissible environment to provide nursing care. It was a marked departure from the institutionalism of the past: the simple, non-labyrinthine floor-plan with short domestic-scale corridors, the study rather than a nurses' station, the orientation to the neighbourhood, including street addresses, the kitchen as a focus and activity area, the fireplace as a conversational focus, the choice of rooms for socialising or for privacy. Years later, these features are increasingly seen as best practice in dementia design.

The kitchen as the focus of the home is a feature in virtually all of the case studies presented in this book. While the method of food preparation varies in the various houses, great efforts have been made to have individual kitchen facilities and adjacent dining rooms. In some the food preparation occurs elsewhere and is delivered by "cook-chill" or similar processes (e.g. Sidegate Lane; Flynn Lodge, The Village, Inglewood and Moorside); in others, everything occurs in-house (all of the Scandinavian and Finnish examples and The

Meadows in Sydney). Clearly the desire to facilitate normality, homeliness, and encouraging domestic activities which promote independence means that as much cooking as possible should occur within each dwelling.

The idea of "home" must, by definition, be culturally appropriate. In Tampere, Finland they have an in-house sauna rather than a bath, something with which the residents are perfectly familiar. Appropriate there, it would certainly be unusual and disorientating elsewhere. In the northern hemisphere, the colder climate means that the gardens are almost invariably smaller and there are fewer external activities. Australia is much more temperate and more oriented to the outdoors all year round. The CADE unit at Riverview Lodge has a simple garden where residents can safely walk, tend the garden or sit. ADARDS nursing home in Tasmania has yard areas with chickens, birds, dogs and cats. Collecting the eggs, watching the fowls and washing or polishing the car are daily activities which many residents have been doing all their lives.

Flynn Lodge in the Northern Territory recognises that, for indigenous people, "home" is as much the external spaces as the building itself; indeed the building is almost a support act to the Australian "great outdoors", providing shade from the sun and a place to put valuable possessions.

Other case studies have expressed "home" in other ways. Kinross in Western Australia has comfortable lounge rooms whose furnishings – armchairs, curtains, light fittings, works of art and old wireless set – are of a bygone era. The simple act of taking your shoes off at the front door in a Swedish "group living" is making a statement that this is "home". Sidegate Lane is notable among all the case studies in that, like most of the surrounding houses it has no "name", only an address.

Personal identification with the environment significantly enhances the sense of familiarity and feeling that this place is indeed "home". That sense of personal identity is achieved in many different ways, but the most recurring theme in these case studies is the use of the residents' own belongings. In bedrooms the use of the resident's own bed, bedside table, dresser, "precious" things, even a small refrigerator have been commonly used. In one case a picture rail in each bedroom has been used to display special personal effects and memorabilia.

Probably the most contentious of these personal items is the bed: should they be provided for residents or should they bring their own? Moorside in Winchester; Impivaarakoti in Tampere and Riverview Lodge in Wingham have opted for the first approach; others are quite insistent that people should bring their bed with them because it is a central piece of furniture with which they identify (e.g. The Meadows in Sydney, the Swedish "group livings"; Parkside in Melbourne).

The therapeutic decision to encourage as much personal furniture as possible has significant design implications: if the bedrooms are too small or have difficult shapes, it will be simply impossible to accommodate the personal effects of residents.

3. The environment must be legible

A user or resident of any building should be able to "read" the building. That expectation is even more important when people have a cognitive disability caused by Alzheimer's or another form of dementia.

Apart from achieving an enabling environment for people with dementia through being small and familiar, it is vital that it is also both orientating and understandable. This legibility is expressed in four ways.

The first, and most critical, is "visual access" – the capacity of the residents to see or sense where they are – or want to go. Different case studies have featured this in a number of quite distinct and varied ways. Riverview Lodge at Wingham in New South Wales is an example of the Australian CADE units which were the first units to give expression to the concept of "total visual access". All of the bedrooms open onto the lounge and dining area; there are no corridors. The same design solution is found in the cottages at The Village in Perth, Australia.

Elsewhere others have sought to provide visual access in an environment with corridors. Both Hasselknuten in Stenungsund, Sweden with its "L" shape and The Meadows with its "Y"-shaped cottages are good examples, with total visual access from all parts of the building. Lindern in Oslo and Moorside in Winchester are two examples where either the remodelling of the building (the former) or the constraints of the site (the latter) made it impossible to have visual access which was total. Both buildings have curved corridors with the communal areas in the middle of the house, solutions which cleverly mean that, while there are points within the house that you cannot see where you want to go, you can nonetheless sense it.

Total visual access is also a key design issue which impacts upon care management. The corollary of residents having good visual access from all parts of the building is that staff can see where residents are.

An important component in that legibility is also ensuring that there are no "dead ends" or, at the very least, their minimisation. It is important to ensure that, if decision points in wayfinding must be made, every decision is a "right one". Where dead ends cannot be avoided, as at Lindern in Oslo, they are minimised.

The second means, cueing, is a very close design ally of visual access. Cueing is to people with dementia what navigational lights are for aviators, providing the encouraging and confirming clues to assist wayfinding. If visual access is the device by which residents get to communal living or external areas, cueing may be the means by which they succeed in getting back. In the words of Brian Kidd, cueing means that "the design uses the building as a language".

The majority of the case studies use some forms of redundant – or passive – cueing: the use of different timber panels or beading for doors; the use of distinctive architectural features, such as emblems or decals on the back door of the house; the use of strategically placed furniture such as a flower box; the placement of bedroom doors and windows to individualise rooms; the strategic use of natural lighting and identifiable architectural details. More active cueing includes landmarking such as a framed collection of memorabilia or a decorated name at a bedroom door.

However, while most facilities have used visual cues such as these, the number of examples of cueing which have used the other senses are fewer. Aldersgate uses a bell to signify the front door; many other places recognised the importance of the sounds and smells of the kitchen to assist wayfinding. Hasselknuten in Stenungsund, Sweden strategically and consciously used different floorings – with their attendant feels and sounds – as cueing for the kitchen, laundry and bedrooms, a fact which is all the more pronounced when moving around the apartment in socks or stockinged feet. Parkside in Melbourne, one of the most vigorous users of redundant cueing, consciously used changes in wall and floor textures in an attempt to compensate for its challenging re-modelled floor plan. The other Scandinavians used tactile wall hangings while The Meadows used different bedroom door handles.

Cueing works hand-in-hand with visual access for continence management in many designs. Ensuring that the toilet can be seen from the bed in rooms with en suites; ensuring that en suite toilets have down lights to direct attention to them; ensuring that toilets in living areas are distinctively landmarked: all of these devices are used in these case studies to enhance successful continence management outcomes. What was also interesting was that there was an almost complete absence of control in the cueing. Residents of these homes were not without choice. Rather the cues helped that choice – and whatever was chosen, it was almost invariably successful.

While colour was used in some cueing schemes, there was an increasing conviction expressed within the case studies that colour, of itself, was an inadequate cueing device. Certainly the yellowing of the eye's lens with age means that there is an unevenness in the perception of colour among residents. But the case studies encouraged the use of multi-sensory cueing, rather than reliance on visual cues alone. If, as Brian Kidd suggests, the design uses the building as a language we will in the future see an enhancement of its vocabulary well beyond the visual.

Different spaces or rooms for different functions will assist legibility. Most of the examples in this book have resisted the temptation to have "multi-purpose" rooms. For people with cognitive impairment, changing the use of the room works against orientation. Rather we see in these examples a variety of small spaces with discrete functions: quiet places to sit, either in private or together (e.g. Flynn Lodge); separate dining areas, even different places to eat according to the meal or occasion to assist in time orientation (e.g. Impivaarakoti, Tampere).

But if you do not have "multi-purpose" rooms, where do you have one-off or occasional activities? Both The Village at Inglewood and Kinross have activity or club rooms, which are separate from the cottages, to which residents go for events, be they games, concerts or social functions. With far greater site constraints, Moorside has an activities room which is on the ground floor and Lindern has a day care centre on another floor. The virtue of such separate facilities is that the resident has a choice of involvement: activities or social occasions are not thrust into their home.

The design must enhance orientation by highlighting important stimuli and reducing the impact of extraneous stimuli. The prosthetic environment compensates for the individual's dysfunction. A dizzying array of stimuli will promote confusion and disorientation. The design challenge is to ensure that the environment is engaging without being confusing; directive without being manipulative; supportive while still promoting autonomy.

It has been said that "noise is to people with dementia what stairs are to people in wheelchairs." The design

and location should promote the possibility of a calm, quiet environment in which the number of unfamiliar faces and alarming noises are minimised. Riverview Lodge is a simple example of this approach: on the banks of a river, on the outskirts of a country town, with residents having to cope with few unfamiliar faces. The connecting walkway at The Meadows is more sophisticated, with all of the building's laundry and other services delivered through the walkway.

4. The environment should promote self-esteem, autonomy and individuality.

We have already seen that this has the implication of requiring larger personal spaces to fit familiar, personal belongings. But it also has other implications.

First, there must be plenty of capacity to fulfil activities of daily living. You might be entertained in a theatre; you might be waited upon in a restaurant or hotel. But in our own homes we occupy our time with activities of daily living: food preparation, cleaning, putting out the washing, listening to the radio or watching the television; polishing the car; or tending the garden. In designing the building, these activities must be taken into account. It is difficult to import them later if, for example, there is no laundry, no provision for food preparation or no garden for residents to be involved in.

One of the greatest challenges is to ensure that there is provision for the activities of men as well as women. ADARDS in Tasmania has its chickens and a car to wash, as mentioned above. A number of places have tool sheds and many places encourage gardening. In the Swedish examples residents are able to smoke in their bedrooms or outside.

There must be external spaces which are both pleasant and safe. The CADE units like Riverview Lodge were forerunners in providing accessible garden areas and virtually all of the Australian examples have generous external areas. Residents are not cooped up inside. Even our case studies in far less temperate locations, such as Impivaarakoti in Tampere, Finland and ADARDS in Hobart have good external spaces. Moreover, they must be spaces which are not "precious objects", but spaces in which residents can be happily, even energetically involved. Sidegate Lane has pleasant gardens and the raised planter boxes allow full involvement in the gardening by residents.

It must be an environment which welcomes and encourages relatives and visitors. There is a clear tension between controlling the level of stimuli and ensuring that the environment does not become a maximum security prison. But the case studies are replete with features which accommodate both features. Most have achieved it by ensuring that there are places for residents and visitors to be together without disturbing other residents – and without using their bedrooms. Sidegate Lane has a large formal lounge room and conservatory; the gardens in most Australian examples allow visiting grandchildren to play safely; the kitchen areas in most facilities allow visitors to involve themselves in making refreshments, while the provision of many different sitting areas allows quiet conversation.

All of these case studies have encouraged strong relationships with the external community. This is expressed simply but importantly as the buildings looking like the rest of the surrounding neighbourhood. Clearly this is achieved in the re-modelled examples, such as Anton Pieckhofje in The Netherlands, Hasselknuten in Sweden, Lindern in Oslo and Parkside in Melbourne. But newer buildings, such as Impivaarakoti in Finland and the Perth examples, have worked hard to reflect the neighbourhood.

But the issue of community interface is not simply an issue of façade. It is a question of relationship. Some designs, not in this book, attempt to create a community environment within the dementia facility: corridors are stylised architecturally as pseudo-streets, personal bedrooms are "pretend houses" and it is all hermetically sealed in an isolated, alienating, unreal and unhomely environment which is little more than a maximum security prison. It is vital that the design enables relationships with the external community. Certainly Snipan, next door to a child daycare centre and on the ground floor of a block of apartments enables this; certainly Moorside, with its proximity to the inner city community of Winchester, enables residents to readily go to the local bingo or delicatessen; certainly Anton Pieckhofje and Lindern are similar. Certainly, 248 Sidegate Lane makes a strong statement of relating to its community by using its street address as its name. The important factor is that the design at least makes such relationships with the external community possible.

"Control mechanisms" must be minimised and unobtrusive. Staff and organisations have a duty of care. It is also vital that the dignity, privacy and independence of the resident be respected. These two, sometimes competing imperatives mean that it is important that forms of control are minimised and those that are necessary are made as unobtrusive as possible. Locked doors have been kept to a minimum in these case studies; some homes use reed switches for external doors (e.g Flynn Lodge); mimic panels (e.g. ADARDS and Riverview Lodge) and computerised passive infra-red systems (e.g. Meadows and Kinross) are used to ensure various levels of intelligent "management by exception"; and many facilities have remote switches for kitchen appliances.

5. The environment must be safe

The environment must ensure that both the residents and the staff are safe. In many environments built for people with dementia, this theme is unfortunately the overriding one, with the result that much effort is put into alarms, secure boundaries, locked doors and the like. It is an outcome which may fulfil the duty of care, but struggles to promote independence, autonomy and dignity.

Of course, there must be round-the-clock security from external intrusion. This is primarily an occupational health and safety issue. Security must be perceived as well as real. The risk will vary according to the site of the facility: it is less in the smaller towns and cities and greater in a larger metropolis. Many of these case studies are fenced and front doors are locked. However, for centres with a number of smaller, separate cottages, the challenge is the security of their staff moving between cottages at night. ADARDS in Tasmania has resolved this by opening up the doors to the units at night. Staff at Moorside, Sidegate Lane and Lindern can move from level to level; staff at The Meadows have the covered walkway to move between the cottages and the administration block.

Of course, residents should be able to walk and stroll securely. The promotion of dignity and independence of the residents must be balanced against the sometimes competing imperative of the duty of care of staff and the organisation. There are considerable cultural variations in how this tension has been addressed: in Australia, a higher premium is placed upon security from wandering and virtually all of the case studies are fenced. This is less of a design feature in the Scandinavian and Finnish examples. Whether this is because fences are an integral part of white Australian culture, or because Australians are more fearful of litigation, is an intriguing and as yet unresolved issue.

Of course, residents should be safe from injuring themselves in the home. This has been achieved in a variety of ways by the case studies, including: warm water systems and colour-coded taps to prevent scalds; safety-grab rails and non-slip flooring to minimise falls; remote switches for kitchen appliances and reverse cycle or convection heating to prevent fire or burns; sharp knives, medicines and detergents in secure cupboards to prevent cuts and poisoning

Finally, the residents must be able to be assisted, particularly at night. For most dementia residents, a traditional nurse call system is both institutional and of little use. An alarm system is confusing and upsetting. ADARDS in Tasmania have again resolved this by opening the facility up at night with motion detectors connected to mimic panels; The Meadows and Kinross use a pager-based computerised infra-red monitoring system which is interconnected to the fire detection systems.

All of these facilities comply with the differing building codes for smoke and fire detection. But so do many poorly designed buildings. The challenge is to do so creatively and in a non-institutional way.

Safety is an important priority. But it must be balanced against the other four key themes that we have identified in these case studies. The keynote is not the elimination of risk, but its management.

Conclusion

At the beginning of this chapter we suggested the dual objectives of designing for people with dementia were to provide an environment which *(i)* promoted improvement and *(ii)* compensated for the individual dysfunction of residents.

The case studies in this book, which come from eight countries, have been successful in their endeavour to achieve this sort of environment. They are separated by distance, by language, by culture, by climate, and by laws. They are all different, with distinctive features. And yet their smallness and sensitivity to scale; their focus upon familiarity, as culturally appropriate homes with which the residents can personally identify; their legibility, being understandable and orientating; their promotion of self-esteem, autonomy and individuality; and their appreciation of safety, within an environment of manageable risk demonstrate that providing the best physical environment for people with dementia is not a question of money or luck, but of good, thoughtful, client-concerned design.

Design for Dementia

Interpreting 'home', the architect's dilemma

By Peter Phippen

ALL THE BUILDINGS illustrated in this book have been visited by one of the contributors, the majority by two and a number by all three.

The writer of this piece visited all the mainland European examples, all the UK buildings with one exception but only one Australian. The comments are therefore Euro-centred, for which I apologise to Australian colleagues in particular. I hope that it is countered by two factors. Firstly, the very comprehensive coverage of Australian projects in the body of the book. Secondly, by the fact that I am using European examples to describe an approach.

Each scheme is illustrated in a standard format including floor plans, internal and external photographs. Statistical information covering staffing, management, technical and cost information is also provided. In a few instances there are unavoidable gaps in the presentations.

Generally the buildings illustrated are modest. There are no attempts at making architectural statements. They are also situated "in the community". This is particularly true of the Scandinavian examples. Even where they are located on a hospital campus they are close to the surrounding roads and streets.

The two characteristics above, that of modest architectural intent and location in the community, are to an extent interlinked. If accommodation is located in the community then the facilities used by the community can be used by residents. There is no need to provide within the building such facilities as a street, a shop or a restaurant. The theory of doing so was much admired by architects at least in the recent past but the idea has more recently been seriously questioned for two reasons. Firstly and very obviously, on cost grounds. To provide such facilities uses valuable space. Buildings are expensive to build, they are also expensive to service and to maintain and in a large part of Europe, at least, to heat. Secondly on the grounds that it is better, more therapeutic, for people to go out or be taken out into the *real* world, to *real* shops and to *real* restaurants for just as long as they are able.

Common purpose, climatic and cultural differences

It is perhaps worth reflecting on the fact that although all the buildings were designed specifically to provide residential accommodation, a "home" for dementia sufferers, there are considerable differences of approach.

To begin with there are major climatic differences, the Northern Territories in Australia with average temperature of 30 degrees Celsius and 30mm precipitation per annum, to Helsinki in Finland with temperatures down to 10 degrees and 80mm precipitation, and London 15 degrees and 70mm precipitation. This, not surprisingly, results in very different buildings and very different attitudes to outside space.

There are other differences, cultural ones reflecting people's aspirations relating to interior finishes, to the way meals are prepared and taken and others relating to what constitutes a normal and desirable residential building and lifestyle. For example, the Australian bungalow with its front and back yards and the French urban apartment block.

Domestic characteristics

The challenge for architects and designers can perhaps, then, be defined as to provide a domestic or "homely" environment in which therapeutic care can be delivered easily, efficiently and economically in a building which in no way signals externally its effectively institutional function.

It is possible to analyse design and design decisions against the characteristics of both a "homely environment", and an environment designed to be more positively therapeutic and to understand the issues which affect this. Also to analyse and understand what creates or avoids the appearance of an institution.

This analysis is possible in the choice of site, in the planning of buildings, in the facilities provided and in the interior design. Below, the characteristics of siting, entrances, kitchens and dining arrangements of the schemes illustrated are reviewed but the approach can and should be extended to cover all aspects of interior and exterior design.

Domestic characteristics – siting

The design of such an environment starts with the choice of site.

Of the twelve European examples:

- one, Impivaarakoti, is a single house set on its own plot virtually indistinguishable from its neighbours;
- two, Hasselknuten and Snipan, are on the ground floor of large apartment blocks;
- two are on healthcare sites, Woodlands and Annalakoti + Pekkalakoti, although the latter, comprising two linked buildings, is in a suburban residential area;
- two, Lindern and Moorside, are on busy streets in urban areas.

The position of the building on the plot is important. Sidegate Lane, although in a residential suburb, is set well back from the road and so appears different from the surrounding houses, an institution, school, hospital department, or clinic perhaps. The only view of the larger outside world is of the car park from the conservatory adjoining the entrance which is remote from the residential clusters.

At Moorside all living rooms overlook the street and dining rooms overlook the garden. This provides residents with a direct visual link to the community and the world outside.

If the therapeutic value of "ordinariness" is to be established, we need to be careful where we site buildings in the community, and where we place them on the particular site, in order that they conform with the residential norm. In a suburban residential setting in the UK this usually means behind a shallow front garden. A large parking area fronting the road or street with the building set well back on the site is out of character and sends institutional signals. Elsewhere, similar tests should be applied: Is it the normal residential arrangement in the particular locale?

Domestic characteristics — entrances

If the siting of the building gives an important preliminary impression of the nature of the building, the entrance gives an even stronger foretaste of what is in store for the visitor or resident. In individual buildings like Impivaarakoti the solution is obvious but where residential clusters are grouped a decision has to be made between individual entrances and a shared one. At Annalakoti + Pekkalakoti, two clusters/21 residents, individual entrances are maintained; at Sidegate Lane, three residential clusters/24 residents, there is an impressive foyer and a generous communal lounge, all rather hotel like in character. At Lindern, two residential clusters/15 residents, access is direct into each each floor from a common staircase. At Moorside there is a small foyer and reception area which also serves the day centre. At Hasselknuten the entrance is shared with other "family" flats.

The type of entrance generally results from whether or not centralised services are provided. A central kitchen and a central laundry (all UK schemes and Les Parentèles) results in a building with a central circulation "core" to provide access to those services. The provision of this "core" allows the provision of other facilities, a lounge for all the residents (Sidegate Lane), a medical room (Moorside and Les Parentèles), a hairdressing salon (Moorside and Woodlands).

Domestic characteristics — provision of shared spaces

There are wide variations in the provision of shared spaces in the schemes illustrated. For example:

Impivaarakoti is run, apparently very successfully, as though the residents were a big family. There is very little or no scope for residents to see visitors, relatives or friends in private. Neither is there space for staff; it really appears to function as one big family. A similar approach is also adopted in the Swedish *gruppeboende* but the communal spaces are more generous and subdivided.

Sidegate Lane is very different. Housing twice as many people as Impivaara and as many as three times the number in a typical Swedish *gruppeboende*, it divides them into three groups or clusters, each with its own living/dining room but also providing a generous amount of additional shared space, a foyer, a communal lounge and a conservatory. Whatever else this does, it sends clear signals to relatives and visitors that the residents are living in very comfortable, if not stylish, conditions. It also provides a very pleasant venue for

friends and visitors to meet residents and staff in a relaxed, social setting.

At Les Parentèles small rooms are provided for each cluster which enables friends and relatives to meet with residents or staff. But small sparsely furnished rooms visited only occasionally for a special purpose, although introducing privacy do not facilitate relaxed exchanges. Other similar spaces in the building are equipped as a play room for child visitors, as a dining room for visitors and as a music room.

Anton Pieckhofje is planned around an internal courtyard which residents' relatives have planted and landscaped and also maintain. This is something made possible by the building's location, in the middle of a residential area with, no doubt, a high proportion of local residents. Shared accommodation is totally separate from the (very autonomous) flats and comprises an office and meeting room.

Domestic characteristics – kitchens

Where residential clusters are autonomous and food is prepared within the cluster a circulation "core" is less important. This automatically results in a less institutional character than where centralised provision is made. Scandinavian examples, a number of Australian ones and Anton Pieckhofje are run on this principle, which is a fundamental one in generating a "homely", domestic character and a participatory and therapeutic culture.

Providing a regime which positively supports the skills residents retain is essential and the kitchen and the preparation of food is central to this. The kitchen can be the place where the barriers between carer and cared for are taken down.

Kitchen design and planning varies greatly from the "farmhouse" kitchen, a room with the space for a large dining table (Hasselknuten and Snipan) to kitchens which form part of a larger space including dining facilities. At Lindern the kitchen is a domestic-sized space separated from the dining room by a counter and high level cupboards. The dining room has separate tables and manages to create the character of a small restaurant or coffee shop.

The common arrangement in Australia is for the kitchen area to be separated from the dining area by a counter with a work surface at normal height on the kitchen side and a low table-height breakfast bar on the dining side. Residents can sit at the bar, have snacks and talk to whoever is working in the kitchen. At The Meadows the kitchen can be shut off from the dining room with a shutter. One of the nice things with open kitchen arrangements is that cooking smells can permeate the group or cluster, a way of enriching the lives of people who are generally deprived of much normal sensory stimulation.

Domestic characteristics – dining arrangements

Eating arrangements largely stem from where food is prepared. For example, at Hasselknuten and Snipan, each with a total of six residents, and at Impivaarakoti, with 13 in total, there is a large dining table which everyone sits around. At Les Parentèles, with six clusters each with ten residents, the kitchen in each cluster (largely a servery as there is a central kitchen) is an enclosed room with separate dining tables for small groups within the large living room.

Design for Dementia

Domestic characteristics – personal space

In Finland, a major provider, Sopimusvuori, appears to have opted, positively, for double rooms in their latest scheme. The reason they state is that their residents prefer them; the majority of people have shared a room with someone for most of their lives and prefer to continue to do so. There is of course the fact that they will have shared it with someone they have chosen and wanted to share with.

However, there is a view, usually a covert one, that individual rooms are really for the benefit of relatives rather than always for the benefit of the individual. Could there be a case therefore for making rooms large enough to take two single beds or for making it possible to link rooms?

There is the real danger with the former approach that at some stage in the future "officialdom" and/or finance directors will realise that each room is potentially a double and it will become one from then on. It would be a pity if such an arrangement could not be managed in the best interests of residents.

Night-time cover and servicing

A fundamental reason for providing a central circulation "core" and which has a fundamental impact on running costs is in order to provide efficient and economic night-time care. There are a number of examples where this is combined with individual access to residential clusters: ADARDS, where there are four wings around a central "hub" which provides a nurses' station for night-time use, and Lindern, where each flat is entered off a common stair. Both arrangements enable shared night-time cover.

The Meadows is special in several ways. It consists of three bungalows each housing 12 or 14 residents. The residents are divided into two clusters sharing a living room, a dining room and a kitchen and laundry.

The entrance to each bungalow is straight from the street through a front garden, front yard in Australia, to a front porch and a typical "house" front door. There is a small entrance hall of domestic proportions which leads into the large living and dining rooms.

The bungalows are connected to the administrative bungalow, to the nurses' station for night-time cover, and to the service and delivery area by means of an enclosed corridor. This also provides a garden wall and screens the back yard of each bungalow from its neighbours. The service corridor provides access for staff, including maintenance staff, and for the delivery of laundry and supplies into the service area at the rear of the kitchen. This enables the running of each bungalow to go on without residents being disturbed by strangers or disconcerting events.

Servicing arrangements have a significant effect on site planning. Arrangements for storage of refuse, particularly if there is a central kitchen, have to be properly provided and, even if kitchens are provided for individual clusters, bulk storage of refuse may be necessary.

Generic plan arrangements

Looking at the plans of individual buildings there are at least three or four basic plan forms in use. These can be thought of as being "U", "L", "Y" and "I" shaped.

Firstly, the original CADE-inspired "U" shape. The bedrooms are arranged around the central living area and other important characteristics, particularly a recog-

nisably domestic environment, are perhaps traded off in the interests of complete visual access.

The "L" shape, as used at Hasselknuten and Woodlands, provides good visual access. Hasselknuten is particularly interesting in that the visual access is complemented by the use of daylight. The gradation in lighting from the necessarily darker spaces at the ends of the two short corridors to the pool of light at the entrance to the communal areas, providing a visual "magnet", works very well.

The Meadows also has an "L" shaped plan but it has been extended to form a "Y". The stem of the "Y" contains the kitchen, laundry and service spaces and connects to the service corridor. The double-banked corridors forming the arms of the "Y" terminate in small glazed-in porches, attractive, conservatory-like spaces, which give access to garden areas.

Linear, or "I" plans are used in three schemes. At Snipan, the conversion of existing flats produces very generous areas and a not very compact plan with individual rooms arranged along one side of a corridor. This gives views of a courtyard garden along its length.

At Lindern and Moorside, where the bedrooms are arranged on both sides of the corridor with living and dining rooms opposite each other on either side, a visual attraction is provided by means of an area of daylight in the centre of the plan. Interestingly, both corridors, solely due to site constraints, are curved on plan which makes them more interesting and improves visual access to one or other of the day spaces.

Interior planning and design

The internal character of the building is dependent on the plan form, the size and scale of the spaces, the quality of daylighting and artificial lighting, the type of finishes (not only their appearance but their texture and sound absorbency) and the style and character of the furniture and fittings.

National characteristics are an important element here. In the UK carpeted floors are seen as a prerequisite of creating a domestic environment. Consequently carpet cleaning is a major activity. In France, it being a Mediterranean country, there is an acceptance, or perhaps liking, for hard, tiled floor finishes combined with generous spaces and volumes as being traditional, particularly in the south. Perhaps for the same reason French artificial lighting often lacks contrast and is bright to the point of being glaring. Les Parentèles has those characteristics which to British eyes are synonymous with institutions. I suspect they are more normal to French people and perhaps merely suggest a rather upmarket style of interior.

However, there is another important issue for architects which is the question of "style". Architects have for many years been trained to think that buildings have to be "modern", use modern materials, with clean plain surfaces and minimal details. The result can be marvellous and exciting: Sydney Opera House or the Lloyds building show this. It can also be bland and boring as is demonstrated in many modern office and institutional buildings throughout the world.

However, in domestic design different criteria apply. The modern "style", for style it is, does not reflect the way most people live and is often in direct conflict with the style of the furniture and furnishings they are familiar with and like. If a "home" environment is to be created, the characteristics of "home" must be clearly recognised.

It is important that designers think about and understand the type of spaces that the people/potential residents will be familiar with and think of as home. This changes with the generations as does the design of equipment people are familiar with. Taps are an obvious example where younger people, the older people of the future, will generally be familiar with lever taps which the present generation of older people demonstrably are not. A similar situation exists with furniture and decor. It is an established fact that people's taste is formed in early adulthood. Therefore what older people like, and are familiar with, changes over the years. This needs to be born in mind when redecoration and the replacement of furniture takes place.

A related issue is one of consistency. Should furniture and decoration be consistent within a scheme or cluster? There is a strong case for variation; it assists orientation and is enriching for people, it increases the pleasure of "visiting". It also, over time, accepts the reality of replacement when items of furniture and equipment go out of production.

What is more permanent is the character of the spaces within buildings. The size of spaces, such as the size of window openings which affects the desire to see without being seen, or the acoustic performance of spaces – an important balance to be struck between hard and soft surfaces to prevent people who are hard of hearing being disorientated – these and similar issues need to be thought about carefully.

Making judgements on what constitutes "homeliness" is a very subjective business. It is the result of one person of a certain age brought up in certain culture within a certain socioeconomic group. It would, however, be surprising if there was not general agreement that the Scandinavian examples rate highly in providing a "home-like" environment.

Impivaarakoti is virtually identical to the houses around it; Hasselknuten and Snipan are converted "family" flats. The internal detailing is therefore domestic. Doors, windows, blinds etc. are all the same as people are used to and have had in their own homes. Larger, institutional buildings have better quality, tougher doors and ironmongery, for good reason. However, this can lead to the loss of the illusion of "home", as surely as if the floor to ceiling heights are too great or the spaces and rooms too large. At worst, non-domestic ironmongery, sanitary ware and taps all confuse people who, often, cannot work out how to use them.

It is very important that architects, designers and particularly clients, are really clear as to what they want to achieve. I would suggest that architects and designers ask themselves what is the character of the building and spaces they are setting out to achieve, and then consider the key attributes of those spaces. I hope that the checklist at the end of this chapter will be helpful.

There are perhaps three possible models for an appropriate caring environment: home, hotel and institution. I would suggest that they have very different characteristics in respect of siting and access, type of entrance, size and scale of spaces, type of finishes and fittings and degree of individual freedom permitted.

A home environment in the UK, for example is usually a one-family house set near to, but not on, the street with its own front door. Internal spaces are tightly planned, floor to ceiling heights low and there is a preponderance of soft furnishings, including fitted carpets throughout, even in bathrooms in many UK homes, producing an absorbent, quiet acoustic which British people regard as an essential part of a "home" environment.

Other attributes which create the feel of home include:
- lighting levels, usually low rather than high and often with a high degree of contrast;
- colour schemes often using restrained and subtle colours with low contrast;
- the use of patterned carpets, fabrics and wall coverings.

The majority of these characteristics would appear to cause older people, and particularly those with dementia, problems. High lighting levels, bolder colours and the absence of patterned floor and wall coverings tend to help people understand the environment in which they live. Add to this the need, in purely functional terms, for a seamless, moisture-resistant, easily-cleaned and non-absorbent floor finish and one has all the characteristics of a typically institutional or even hospital environment. It will need more than a few pictures hung on the walls to correct this impression.

These issues, however, highlight the conflicts between designing a "home" environment and a therapeutic one. It is necessary for architects, designers, managers and carers to balance the requirements of both.

Sometimes simple devices and techniques can be used to maintain an essentially domestic environment. For example, fire extinguishers can be hidden in cupboards (as at The Meadows) with the agreement of the fire authority; or, a decorative line or border can be used on the floor around the edge of a room (Hasselknuten). This very traditional device can run across door openings and so discourage people going through the door. Alternatively, if the line goes through the door, it may encourage people to go through it.

The test must be subjective, but it comes down to which is dominant: if the normal furniture and objects associated with "home" provide the dominant impact then domesticity rules; if the devices of therapeutic need are too obvious, then an institutional character is inevitable.

Cueing

The conflict of views here is clearly demonstrated by attitudes to cueing. The majority of schemes illustrated use cueing devices at least to the extent of having "customised" individual signs on doors to individual rooms. However, in a few schemes, Anton Pieckhofje and Sidegate Lane for example, no cueing devices were used on the grounds that they are not really domestic. After all, you don't have them in your own home.

The design of outside spaces

Outside spaces often leave a lot to be desired. Architects and landscape architects often fail to understand their potential for providing both usable space, sensory stimulation and simply delight.

Views of trees and shrubs measure the seasons. Plants and flowers provide both colour and smell but these need to be directly and closely experienced to maximise their therapeutic effects. To do this there needs to be easy access, security, shelter, sun and shade. Gardens need to be planned and designed as carefully and as expertly as the building. They are not just something to look at, but spaces to be used.

Moorside has a pleasant courtyard garden facing south with a pergola and a perimeter path. Anton Pieckhofje has a central atrium.

Areas properly orientated and designed to provide shelter and shade immediately adjacent to the building can enable residents and staff to sit outside and to engage in therapeutic tasks in surprisingly low air temperatures. Moorside, for example, in mid-March (average daytime temperature 14 degrees Celsius) had a group of residents sitting outside, with carers, engaged in occupational therapy. Such spaces can therefore produce valuable additional space at low cost at the same time making life more enjoyable for residents and for staff.

However, it is the Australian schemes which demonstrate a far more imaginative attitude to outside spaces in the way they are used. For example The Meadows, as well as having a pleasant, sheltered terrace for outdoor living, also has a "back yard" complete with a rotary clothes drier, known universally in Australia by its proprietory name, a "Hills Hoist". This, with the laundry trolley, is a standard piece of equipment used by staff and residents and perhaps a sign of a genuinely participatory culture.

At ADARDS, chickens and a permanently parked car provide continuity with previous lifestyles.

Cost and value for money

Cost, capital cost and running costs are a fundamental consideration in all countries. Group living goes with an acceptance of the need to join groups into a larger complex to allow, in general terms, economies of scale. The exceptions to this, the Swedish *gruppeboende*, were at least partly the result of, or made possible by, a surplus of flat accommodation, a product of earlier government policy.

Unfortunately cost comparisons are complicated by buildings' different completion dates due to the impact of inflation and other economic factors. Comparisons between building costs are notoriously difficult to make across national boundaries.

There are three measures which may help to provide an indication of the efficiency of the planning of the chosen buildings and therefore an idea of value for money. Although given in the Matrix (Appendix B), overall floor area is of less interest than floor area per resident. Perhaps the most useful measures are:
- size of individual rooms;
- shared living space per resident calculated by dividing the floor area of living and dining rooms by the number of people who use them;
- total floor area per person: the total floor area divided between the total number of residents.

Like all statistical information the figures do need interpretation. The floor area per individual room is straightforward. Shared living space per resident is the area of the living space attached to each cluster. Shared living rooms serving groups of clusters are shown separately.

Total floor area per person is dependent on what facilities are included, provision of a medical room, a hairdressing salon, whether or not there is a laundry, will all affect the result.

Design checklist

The following points, a mix of questions and assertions, may help those involved in commissioning and designing new buildings, or remodelling existing ones, to finalise their design briefs and also to understand the implications of some of their basic decisions. It is by no means exhaustive but it is hoped it will assist in providing buildings where there is a good fit between the spaces that are provided and the way they are used.

- Is the site in the community? What facilities are within easy reach? The more the better.

- The position of the new building on the site should respect the building line of adjoining buildings, also their height and scale.

- The detailing and materials should be synonymous with those of "normal" housing in the area, region or country.

- The only external signage should be the name or number of the building as it would be if it was normal residential accommodation.

- Will there be a common entrance to all the clusters in the building or complex of buildings or will each cluster have an individual entrance or both?

- If a common entrance is provided will it take people through the communal spaces if provided? This makes them accessible to visitors and arguably encourages their use

- What communal spaces, i.e. spaces shared between the groups, are to be provided and how will they be used? It is important to remember that buildings are expensive. They have to be furnished, heated, cleaned and maintained. If they are not essential and regularly used they will tend to become neglected and therefore detract from the maintenance of a caring environment.

- What will be the arrangements for cooking? Will food for all or some meals be prepared centrally and distributed to each group or cluster or will it be prepared in each cluster?

- What degree of resident participation is envisaged in the preparation or clearing away of meals?

- Will tables for small groups be provided, effectively a "boarding house" or "restaurant" approach, or will one large table be provided for all the residents in the cluster, a "family approach"?

- Will all meals be taken at the table or tables, or is provision to be made for some form of breakfast bar for snacks?

- If en suite showers are provided what assisted bath provision is necessary? For economic reasons and social ones it should be less than where en suite facilities are not provided. Residents should have the benefit for as long as possible of being able to bath or be bathed in the privacy of their own room.

- The interior design of the building shell, i.e. doors, screens and windows, should be domestic in character and able to harmonise with a wide range of interior decor.

- Every effort should be made to ensure the building is simple and flexible. Buildings are expensive, often demand expensive infrastructure and, if too specifically designed for one use, they can, for a number of reasons, quickly become redundant. The reasons are partly demographic and partly to do with increased aspirations. For example, accommodation for active old people designed and built 25 to 30 years ago in the UK is now no longer required or practical to use or adapt and is being demolished.

  Flexibility does not mean the ability to change a building overnight using only a screwdriver. What it does mean is the ability over, say, a 10 to 20 year cycle to clear out as required existing walls and partitions to remodel the spaces to suit new requirements and, very importantly, to update and reorganise the electrical and mechanical services.

DESIGN
FOR
DEMENTIA

Part II. The homes

Patrick House

- Converted Victorian house in urban setting • Younger client group • Full bathrooms in each unit • Pleasant kitchen and garden in cramped urban setting • Identical to adjoining houses • Conversion of existing building allowed generous space standards

Patrick House
17 Rivercourt Road
London W6 9LD
Tel: 0181 846 9117
Fax: 0181 741 7344

Owner
London Borough of Hammersmith and Fulham

Managing organisation
St Mungo Community Trust

Contact person for further information
Andrew Langford, Patrick House Manager
Tel: 0181 846 9117

Type of building
Residential and nursing home

Architect
Elizabeth A. Swainston
Chartered Architects
60 Chancellors Road
London W6 9RS
Tel: 0181 748 9202
Fax: 0181 748 0253

Resident/client profile
Ambulant and non-ambulant with highly challenging behaviours and levels of confusion.

DESCRIPTION OF BUILDING

Site context
Urban – one of a row of large detached houses in a residential street.

Number of resident beds
Five

Number of respite or assessment beds
None

Details of other overnight accommodation
Each resident has a double sized bedroom with en suite facilities. Residents have double beds for partners and there is also space for a sofa-bed in each bedroom.

Alternatively, guests can stay overnight on sofa beds in the sitting room (as in any family home).

There are no staff bedrooms — staff provide 24-hour waking cover and do not sleep in.

Plan form
One large five-bedroomed family-style house
"An ordinary house in an ordinary street".

Communal and shared spaces for residents
1 sitting room.
1 combined kitchen/conservatory with dining area.
1 assisted bathroom (shared).
1 laundry room (includes domestic washing machine for personal use by residents).
1 passenger lift serving all levels of the house (excluding cellar areas).
Cellar and garage (for storage but not accessed by residents).
Garden and patio area.
All bedrooms with en suite facilities — one communal toilet in assisted bathroom.

Staff facilities, office and administrative space
One small upstairs office with adjoining toilet/shower room. Second office in converted summer house in the rear garden.

Note that the philosophy of care strongly enshrines the principle that the project is the home of the residents in which staff act as professional visitors.

Service and ancillary spaces
In addition to the communal and shared spaces for residents listed above it should be noted that the house is designed as an ordinary family home and is not serviced in the normal way of an institution. All rooms are fully accessible to residents including the kitchen, assisted bathroom and laundry, but excluding the cellar, garage and the two staff offices.

What site constraints or external factors, such as existing buildings or local planning legislation, affected the form and planning of the building?
In order to achieve the "shared family home" design an unusually large property was required for conversion. The building is a substantial, double fronted and detached house, whereas the typical London house is more usually terraced and on a narrow site with a limited number of rooms (commonly two to three per floor). The limit on the capital money available meant that we could only afford a house of this size because it is the last in a row of houses before the street is bisected by a busy highway feeding central London.

The installation of secondary double glazing to original windows and double glazed units to new windows has reduced the noise level from the nearby highway to "acceptable urban" level.

The roof construction and existence of a cellar were sufficient to allow the installation of a passenger lift without altering the external appearance of the building – which would not have been acceptable to the planning authority.

Construction and external materials
The house is about 90 years old, traditionally built with solid grey brick walls, painted timber sash windows, timber floors and a pitched roof covered in natural slate. The new conservatory extension has matching brick walls with timber windows and a flat roof with short glazed pitches on two sides.

Patrick House looks like just another family house in a street of similar buildings.

Type(s) of flooring
The house is carpeted throughout with Gradus Genus impervious-backed carpet except in wet areas (bathrooms and laundry) where Altro flooring has been used: Marine where people will be in bare feet and Walkway where a safety floor is required but where people will be wearing shoes. The kitchen/conservatory area (includes dining area) has recently been recovered in an equivalent sheet material by Tarkett.

Internal finishes
Internal finishes are standard domestic: walls are finished in emulsion paint and woodwork in gloss paint. The sitting room is papered. The assisted bathroom, laundry room, and en suite shower rooms are fully tiled to half-height or door-head-height where necessary. The tiles are simple, with a border or occasional patterned tile. Sound insulation has been incorporated into new partitions throughout the house.

Equipment
Each bedroom has an en suite shower room and a communal assisted bathroom is available with an Arjo Hi-lo Therapy bath and portable hydraulic bath hoist A Stannah Popular PH61/2 4-person passenger lift has been installed which has access both sides and can serve a half landing between the main ground floor and the first floor thereby enabling full access to all floors of the house (excluding cellar area).

The laundry room has an Electrolux Wascator commercial high spin washer extractor with sluice programme and gas heated tumble dryer. There is also a standard domestic washing machine for personal use by residents. To reduce necessary maintenance and the use of detergents a Culligen Aqua Sensor Water Softener has been installed.

The kitchen is fully fitted in standard domestic style with gas hob, electric oven, dishwasher, microwave oven, refrigerator and freezer – residents have full access to the kitchen. All taps, including those in the kitchen, have thermostatic temperature controls to regulate water heat as required.

Radiators throughout the house have covers to prevent accidental burning through direct contact.
Cass Companion 90 Wireless Call system allows residents to summon staff, staff to summon assistance, and for staff to control the exit door to the street if necessary.

STAFFING

Management staff
1.5 per week full-time equivalents (FTE)
Care staff
10.5 FTE
Other staff
One administrator/housekeeper. 0.5 FTE

BUILDING STATISTICS

Site area within site boundaries
360m² plus shared side access to the garage

Ground floor area i.e. "footprint"
162m²

Total floor area
298m²

Floor area of individual units of accommodation

Ground floor bedroom 1	23m²
Ground floor bedroom 2	18.5m²
Half-landing bedroom 3	18m²
First floor bedroom 4	22m²
First floor bedroom 5	21m²

Clockwise from top left: Rear garden conservatory and terrace; Conservatory extension with dining room and terrace; Conservatory extension, kitchen and dining room; A typical bedroom.

Floor area of common living and dining rooms per group or cluster as appropriate (excluding separate circulation space and corridors)

Sitting room	20.5m²
Kitchen/conservatory	34m²
(includes dining area)	

Building cost including fixed equipment, hard and soft landscaping (but excluding loose furniture and fittings and professional fees)

The cost of the building works in October 1992 was £218,000. Most of the building work was zero-rated for VAT.

BUILDING DESIGN

The philosophy of care

Patrick House provides care and accommodation for people with HIV-related brain impairment (AIDS Dementia) who, due to the effects of their brain impairment, are no longer able to live without 24-hour supervision and support.

Hospitals, hospices and long stay mental health wards are not appropriate care facilities for this client group. A care environment is required that is as near to a home as possible where the person can receive flexible and individualised care that promotes dignity, independence and quality of life.

The care at Patrick House is based on a holistic approach and the primary form of care offered is supervision i.e. enabling residents to manage their impairment as independently as possible. The aim is also to meet all other needs as they arise: social, emotional and spiritual care needs as well as full nursing and terminal/palliative care when required.

How was the philosophy expressed in the design of the building?

Both internally and externally the whole appearance of the house is that of a large, ordinary, shared "family" home. Externally, it is indistinguishable from the other houses in the row, thereby giving the appearance on approach of being an ordinary house in an ordinary street.

Internally the design throughout the entire house is that of an ordinary domestic home, giving the feeling of being in someone's private domestic environment. On entry the light and airy hallway with central staircase leads onto the communal living areas, exactly as one would expect to find "at home". All fittings, furniture and design features are "ordinary domestic". Original Victorian features were either retained or restored/reinstated where they had not survived previous conversion work. Specialist features and equipment are either unobtrusive or appear to be ordinary, so that the entire feel of the house is uninstitutional.

Owing to the size of house, the "service" areas are either tucked away (e.g. passenger lift) or are ordinary in location and appearance, though perhaps large (e.g. laundry room and assisted bathroom). To provide fire protection to the staircase, lobbies had to be constructed and these are glazed to bring natural light in wherever possible and also to allow people to be aware of others in the building and for them not to feel isolated. It also allows the staff to keep an unobtrusive watching eye on rooms and residents. A large Velux roof window was inserted into the roof over the staircase to flood the stairwell with light.

The two staff areas are unobtrusively placed (upstairs and in the garden) and appear much like any "office/study at home". There are no "no-go" areas for residents or their visitors and the hub of the house is the attractive kitchen/conservatory area with dining space which opens onto the garden at the rear of the house. Areas of danger in more traditional nursing homes (kitchens and bathrooms for example) are not avoided or "designed for safety" but residents are rather supervised by staff to live with potential danger exactly as they would be by a personal carer at home. In addition to having full use of the communal and "service" areas, residents have their own (lockable) private double bedrooms with en-suite facilities.

The philosophy of care is therefore supported by an environment which is in every respect the home of the residents, to which their relatives and friends can have full access in the ordinary way, and in which the staff attend as "professional visitors" as if the individual were receiving a 24-hour package of care at home.

Siting
An ordinary house in a residential street close to the shops and facilities of Hammersmith's main shopping street, an underground station, bus routes and a local park, and a short walk in the other direction to gardens and a riverside walk overlooking the Thames with popular riverside pubs. There is easy access to a range of local HIV services and the main London hospitals.

Plan form
The large family house has been maintained at the same time as providing high quality amenities. The bedrooms have en-suite level access shower rooms and all the shower rooms have good natural light.

External character and appearance
The house looks to be nothing more than a family house in a street of family houses and flats.

Approach and entrance
Pathways approach the front entrance door from both corners of the front boundary, one stepped and the other gently ramped, which gives a little more privacy at the front door (assisted by front garden growth) than is afforded by a path at 90 degrees to the pavement.

Approach to signage and cueing
Because the house is small, compact and the planning simple to understand, no provision was made for signage so as to keep the family home atmosphere. The designers were also aware that requirements would change according to individual resident need. Since opening, practice has proved that signage is undesirable as it only serves to enhance dependence and

worsen memory loss and confusion for this client group, rather than encourage residents to maximise their abilities.

Approach to colour schemes and interior design
The decorations and fittings were chosen to provide a homely and lively atmosphere, and since opening, the choice of colour schemes during redecoration has reflected the choices of the personalities involved, as occurs in any domestic setting.

Security provisions
From an external point of view the exterior doors of the property (including driveway gates and side garden door) and all windows are secured against burglaries etc. in the normal way. There is a standard entryphone at the front door but access to this is open from the street via the small front garden. At the side of the house a heat sensitive light is secured to deter unwanted entry over the side garden door. The garden is bordered by neighbours' gardens on three sides in the normal way, and by a head-height brick wall on the side bordering the public pathway which runs alongside the nearby highway on that side of the house.

From an internal point of view the front and back doors are not kept locked, leaving residents free to come and go as they wish, but these doors are connected to the staff call system who are therefore automatically informed when someone enters or leaves the property.

As in a family home, no internal doors are lockable other than the staff office (occasionally required) and cellar access. Bedroom and bathroom doors are not locked but can be bolted by residents from the inside to provide privacy with a simple emergency release from the outside if necessary.

Heating and/or ventilation system or air conditioning system
Gas-fired boilers provide central heating and hot water. All radiators have low surface temperature covers and all have thermostatic valves for individual setting. The sitting room has, in addition, an electric log-effect fire to give a focus to the room. In very hot weather, use is made of free-standing standard domestic electric fans to assist with ventilation if required.

Technology used
There is no specialist technology other than that described above. The technology used is therefore similar to that one might expect to find in many nursing homes not specialising in dementia care. Dementia is managed by staff input rather than by specialist technology or design.

Success in meeting intentions
We are extremely satisfied with the completed building which entirely complements our philosophy of care i.e. the building provides an ordinary domestic "non-institutional" environment in which people can live and receive care exactly as they would at home.

Major hurdles that had to be overcome or prevented the intentions from being achieved
There were very few. Most of the design problems were overcome by finding a house large enough, at an affordable cost, which had sufficient space to allow for the design intentions.

Given the small number of bedspaces, planning permission was not required to convert the property to a registered home, and therefore the public debate over the establishment of a local "AIDS hospice" (a very contentious issue even in the 1990s) was circumvented (and there have been no problems with neighbours since opening).

The registration authorities have occasionally needed some persuasion in some areas e.g. the unlocked front door, the fact that staff do not have a designated rest/eating area separate from the rest of the house, and where unimaginative interpretation of health and safety regulations appear to conflict with domestic design intentions. None of this has presented

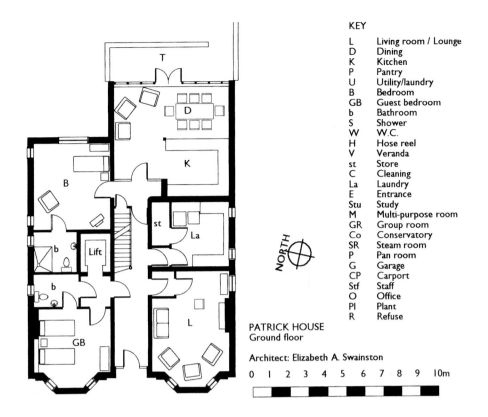

KEY

L	Living room / Lounge
D	Dining
K	Kitchen
P	Pantry
U	Utility/laundry
B	Bedroom
GB	Guest bedroom
b	Bathroom
S	Shower
W	W.C.
H	Hose reel
V	Veranda
st	Store
C	Cleaning
La	Laundry
E	Entrance
Stu	Study
M	Multi-purpose room
GR	Group room
Co	Conservatory
SR	Steam room
P	Pan room
G	Garage
CP	Carport
Stf	Staff
O	Office
Pl	Plant
R	Refuse

PATRICK HOUSE
Ground floor

Architect: Elizabeth A. Swainston

0 1 2 3 4 5 6 7 8 9 10m

significant difficulties as the authorities have at the same time been extremely supportive of our philosophy and intentions.

Aspects of the building design worthy of replication?

The building is in every way a great success. The house is spacious and luxurious but of ordinary domestic home design with a non-institutional feel throughout. Five years after opening there is nothing of note we would change. On the contrary, the physical environment created is a hugely significant factor in the creation of the holistic care environment we strive to maintain.

To be avoided in the future?

There is nothing to report of any note that we are dissatisfied with in the design of the house. Ideally, we would not have liked to be so close to a busy road, but with double/secondary glazing the noise levels are "acceptable urban" and all the other benefits of the property could not have been achieved elsewhere within the limitations of the capital funding available.

Feedback

Feedback from the people with dementia, their friends and relatives, the staff and other professionals has only been extremely positive. There is overwhelming consensus that the environment is pleasant, appropriate and successful. Contrary to expectations, we are having a very significant success rate in achieving dramatic improvements in levels of dementia with 55 per cent of our client group, and the physical and emotional environment is clearly a very major factor.

EDITORS' COMMENTS

Patrick House is a thought-provoking building in a number of respects. It is an ordinary early twentieth-century house in an ordinary street; nothing externally distinguishes it from its neighbours. Inside it has been converted to an exceptionally high standard for five people with AIDS-related dementia. The rooms are big enough for double beds and each has a large

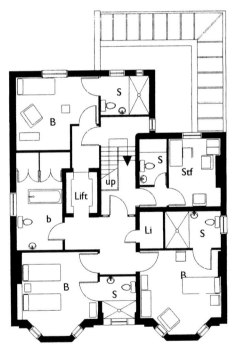

bathroom, with very modern shower controls; age-appropriate for this generation of much younger people with dementia. The exceptionally small scale and the high standards are in marked contrast to many units for older people and expose the ageism rife in so much design for people with dementia.

Patrick House has a big, light kitchen/dining room at the back, opening onto the garden, This is a normal working kitchen again built to an unusually high standard for people with dementia. It has a remarkably non-institutional feel to it. As a family house converted to fit a family living philosophy, it ought to be widely replicated for older people with dementia, for whom it would be eminently suitable.

Hasselknuten

Reasons for selection

- Re-modelled apartments • Good visual access within apartments
- Very large bedrooms • Strategic use of different floorings for cueing
- Eat-in kitchen • Strong identification with neighbourhood

Name and address of building
Hasselknuten
Stenungsund Commune
Svevige
Sweden

Owner
Stenungsund Commune

Contact person for further information
Inga-Britt Johansson
Fax: 0046 303 68060

Type of building
"Gruppeboende" — Flat for group living

Architect
Standburg & Partners

DESCRIPTION OF BUILDING

Site context
Suburban. Adjoins local centre.

Number of resident beds
6

Number of respite/assessment beds or other overnight accommodation
None

Plan form
One ground floor flat

Communal and shared spaces for residents
Day or "family" room with quiet room or "lounge" on one side and "farmhouse" kitchen or dining kitchens on other side. Visually accessible through glazed doors and screens.

Office and administration space and staff facilities
Office/staff room

Service and ancillary spaces
Laundry and sluice room

What site constraints or external factors, such as existing buildings or local planning legislation, affected the form and planning of the building?
Conversion of existing flat building

Construction and external materials
Brick external walls
Type(s) of flooring
Timber parquet in living spaces. Carpet and tiled finishes else-where.

Internal finishes
Plaster finishes generally.

Equipment
No special equipment.

STAFFING
Two staff man the morning shift, another two in the afternoon. One member of staff is on duty at night.

BUILDING STATISTICS

Site area within site boundaries
Not applicable.

Ground floor area i.e. 'footprint'
398m²

Total floor area
398m²

Floor area of individual units of accommodation
33m²

Floor area of common living and dining rooms per group or cluster as appropriate (excluding separate circulation space and corridors)
77m²

Building cost including fixed equipment, hard and soft landscaping (but excluding loose furniture and fittings and professional fees)
Not known

BUILDING DESIGN

The philosophy of care
Aspects of environments, such as the building, furniture and psychological environment are important in the treatment of people with dementia and require knowledge and consideration. A calm, homelike atmosphere is needed where people can feel accepted and can be themselves in a pleasant environment. People affect one another within the group and so it is important that the members of the group relate well to one another.

A good contact with staff, whose specialist knowledge can help an individual to maintain competence is needed. A well planned environment provides the basis for maintenance of competence and the biological functions of the brain. A good environment provides the opportunity to maintain confidence and self-esteem and thus the maintenance of a good quality of life despite dementia.

Hasselknuten: Above, kitchen/dining room;
Below, corridor showing hampers;
Below right, living room with formal dining table
showing the kitchen/dining room to the right.

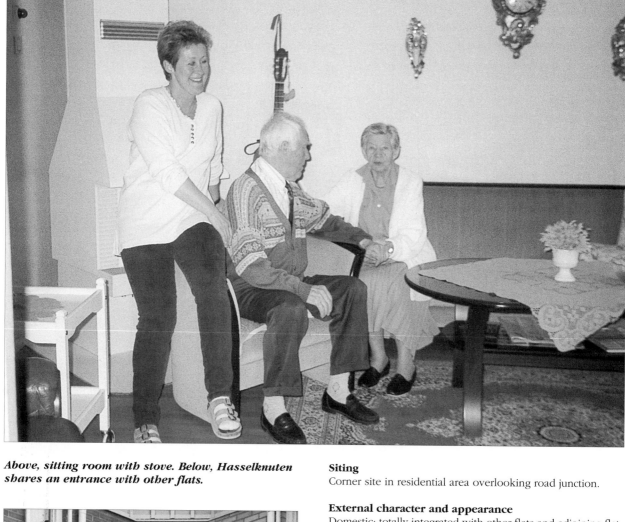

Above, sitting room with stove. Below, Hasselknuten shares an entrance with other flats.

Siting
Corner site in residential area overlooking road junction.

External character and appearance
Domestic; totally integrated with other flats and adjoining flat.

Approach and entrance
Shared entrance hall with other flats.

Approach to signage and cuing
Individual residents information panels on doors to individual rooms with pictures and "objects" on walls to assist wayfinding.

Approach to colour schemes and interior design
Domestic colour schemes and furnishing. Good use of plaques on residents' doors, "tactile" objects and reliefs to assist wayfinding. "Hampers" are used to reduce the apparent length of corridors.

Heating and/or ventilation system or air conditioning system
Low pressure hot water system with radiators. Stove in quiet room or "lounge".

Technology used
No special technology.

EDITORS' COMMENTS
Stenungsund is a new town, near the coast, north of Gothenberg centred around the petrochemical industry. Its character is a typical product of the Scandinavian approach to settlement design consisting very largely of flats in a pleasant landscape setting.

As a result of a concerted effort to solve Sweden's housing problems in the 1970s, over one million flats were built in a

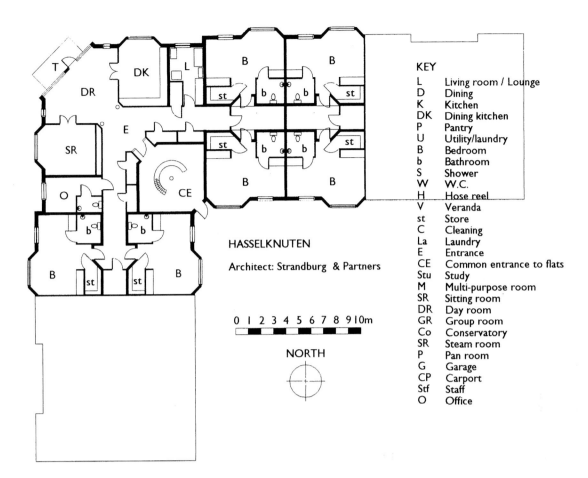

HASSELKNUTEN

Architect: Strandburg & Partners

0 1 2 3 4 5 6 7 8 9 10m

NORTH

KEY

L	Living room / Lounge
D	Dining
K	Kitchen
DK	Dining kitchen
P	Pantry
U	Utility/laundry
B	Bedroom
b	Bathroom
S	Shower
W	W.C.
H	Hose reel
V	Veranda
st	Store
C	Cleaning
La	Laundry
E	Entrance
CE	Common entrance to flats
Stu	Study
M	Multi-purpose room
SR	Sitting room
DR	Day room
GR	Group room
Co	Conservatory
SR	Steam room
P	Pan room
G	Garage
CP	Carport
Stf	Staff
O	Office

very short period. This surplus has been put to good use by creating the "Gruppeboende" or group homes for older people. These generally comprise a series of one-bedroom flats knocked together with one or two flats more radically changed to create the communal areas. The alterations to the flats are kept to a minimum allowing the buildings to be used for a different type of resident in years to come. Each flatlet has a small built-in kitchen an en suite shower/WC and a "walk-in" store. The overall area of each flat is just over 30m². Such conversion is possible because of the simple repetitive nature of the design and the economical approach to planning. (See also Snipan).

Hasselknuten seems a particularly happy example of this approach. It consists of six of these mini-apartments on the ground floor of a small two-storey block of some 12 one-bedroom flats. The entrance is via an hall and staircase lobby which serves other flats not dedicated to dementia care or for older people on the first floor. From the entrance hall immediately inside the front door are the communal rooms, a large day room and on either side of it, separated by glazed screens with double doors, a smaller quiet room and a dining kitchen.

Leading off to left and right are short corridors serving two and four mini apartments. They are broken up by "hampers" or trellises which hang down from the ceiling and reduce the apparent length of the corridors. Pictures and objects adorn the walls and personalised decals the doors to the flats. The need for open and accessible storage to hang outdoor clothes and leave boots in Scandinavian homes also introduces a pleasantly informal note into the entrance hall and corridor spaces.

The location of the the entrance door and entrance to the communal rooms at the pivotal point of the plan not only ensures the plan is immediately comprehensible but also creates a pool of light and provides an attraction when viewed from along the corridors.

This is a deliberately basic description of the plan arrangement, of what is, after all a very simple building. It in no way does justice to how the building feels or what it is like to experience.

Standing inside the entrance door the plan is simple and comprehensible, ahead a family-cum-formal dining room with a large dining table, easy chairs and a piano. It has generous windows and french doors facing south, opening onto a small terrace which overlooks a road junction. The room to the left is, what in most similar buildings would be called a quiet room, a title, redolent with institutional overtones which demonstrates the dangerous power of words. What spaces are called effects the way they are conceived by architects and used by carers. It is of course a sitting room, or perhaps even a snug, complete with stove and built in seating.

The kitchen with a large table is, in English parlance a "farmhouse kitchen", the real centre, where everyone can gather, just like home!

The size of this group, home for six residents, the plan form and the internal design, not "interesting" or "novel" but just appropriate, make Hasselknuten, a special example of a "Gruppeboende" even by the high standards set.

Snipan

- *Re-modelled apartments* • *Good visual access within apartments*
- *Very large bedrooms* • *Strategic use of different floorings for cueing*
- *Eat-in kitchen* • *Strong identification with neighbourhood*

Snipan
Stenungsund Commune
Svevige
Sweden

Owner
Stenungsund Commune

Contact person for further information
Inga-Britt Johansson
Fax: 0046 303 68060

Type of building
"Gruppeboende" – Flat for group living

Architect
Kartekton

DESCRIPTION OF BUILDING

Site context
Urban, near centre of town.

Number of resident beds
6

Number of respite/assessment beds or other overnight accommodation
None

Plan form
One group of six bedsitting rooms each with kitchen and shower room.

Communal and shared spaces for residents
Shared sitting room and kitchen/dining room.

The living room at Snipan provides a calm, homelike atmosphere.

Office/administration space and staff facilities
Small office

Service and ancillary spaces
Storage for each flat, laundry, sluice.

What site constraints or external factors, such as existing buildings or local planning legislation, affected the form and planning of the building?
Existing block of flats.

Construction and external materials
Coloured render and concrete.

Type(s) of flooring
Parquet and tiles.

Internal finishes
Domestic finishes throughout.

Equipment
There is no assisted bathroom, but shavers are provided in each bedsitting room.

STAFFING

Two staff on the morning shift, another two in the afternoon. One member of staff is on duty at night.

The farmhouse-style "eat-in" kitchen at Snipan is an extension of the living room.

BUILDING STATISTICS

Site area
Not applicable.

Ground floor area i.e. "footprint"
606m²
Total floor area
606m²

Floor area of individual units of accommodation
12m²

Left, a typical resident's room. Right, Snipan has individual kitchens in residents' rooms.

BUILDING DESIGN

The philosophy of care

Aspects of environments, such the building, furniture and psychological environment are important in the treatment of people with dementia and require knowledge and consideration. A calm, homelike atmosphere is needed where people can feel accepted and can be themselves in a pleasant environment. People affect one another within the group and so it is important that the members of the group relate well to one another. A good contact with staff, whose specialist knowledge can help an individual to maintain competence is needed. A well planned environment provides the basis for maintenance of competence and the biological functions of the brain. A good environment provides the opportunity to maintain confidence and self-esteem and thus the maintenance of a good quality of life despite dementia.

Siting

Ground floor of block of flats near station and town centre. Identical to other ground floor flats except for separate entrance.

Plan form

Single banked corridor with residents' rooms facing street. Shared living room facing courtyard garden.

External character and appearance

Ground floor of large block of flats. Appear identical to other flats in block.

Approach and entrance

Separate entrance from pavement.

Approach to signage and cuing

Residents "plaques" on doors.

Approach to colour schemes and interior design

Simple domestic decor.

KEY

L   Living room / Lounge
D   Dining
K   Kitchen
P   Pantry
U   Utility/laundry
B   Bedroom
b   Bathroom
S   Shower
W   W.C.
H   Hose reel
V   Veranda
st   Store
C   Cleaning
La   Laundry
Li   Linen
E   Entrance
Stu   Study
M   Multi-purpose room
GR   Group room
Co   Conservatory
SR   Steam room
P   Pan room
G   Garage
CP   Carport
Stf   Staff
Dr   Drugs
Lo   Lockers
Wh   Wheelchairs
O   Office
Pl   Plant
R   Refuse

SNIPAN

Architect: Kartekton

NORTH

0 1 2 3 4 5 6 7 8 9 10m

EDITORS' COMMENTS

Stenungsund is a new town, near the coast, north of Gothenberg centred around the petrochemical industry. Its character is a typical product of the Scandinavian approach to settlement design consisting very largely of flats in a pleasant landscape setting.

As a result of a concerted effort to solve Sweden's housing problems in the 1970s, over one million flats were built in a very short period. This surplus has been put to good use by creating the "Gruppeboende" or group homes for older people. These generally comprise a series of one-bedroom flats knocked together with one or two flats more radically changed to create the communal areas. The alterations to the flats are kept to a minimum allowing the buildings to be used for a different type of resident in years to come. Each flatlet contains a small kitchenette with and en suite shaver room with WC and "walk-in" store. The overall area of each flat is just over 30m². Such conversion is possible because of the simple repetitive nature of the design and the economical approach to planning. (See also Hasselknuten).

Snipan is a Gruppeboende situated on the ground floor of a high rise apartment block which faces south overlooking a main thoroughfare and north overlooking a pleasant courtyard garden. The atmosphere is very different from Hasselknuten because of the plan arrangement and the orientation.

The plan is linear, as opposed to "L" shaped as at Hasselknuten. The entrance is from the street into a wide corridor, an anonymous and undomestic space which leads directly into the living room which has large windows overlooking the courtyard garden. The farmhouse kitchen is an extension of the living room.

Short corridors run off to left and right with mini apartments on the south side and large windows overlooking the garden on the north. The corridors widen to accommodate chairs and small items of furniture. The mini-apartments, therefore, overlook the road and face south and the public areas face north onto the garden.

Residents appear to gravitate to the kitchen which is fully occupied by the large dining table and chairs. The character of Snipan is of a very generous private residence or small hotel with the exception of the kitchen which because of its size (the furniture and fittings are a tight fit) is very "homely".

Design for Dementia

Carntyne Gardens

Reasons for selection

- Plan allows good visual access • Small flats rather than bedrooms • Good access to local shops and facilities • Well-lit circulation areas
- Flats overlook street, communal spaces overlook garden providing variety

Carntyne Gardens
Abbeyhill Street
Glasgow G32 6AB
Tel: 0141 778 4799

Owner and managing organisation
Bield Housing Association Ltd

Contact person for further information
Mr Peter Henshaw
Development Manager
Bield Housing Association
Tel: 0141 333 0700

Type of building
Care centre and sheltered housing

Architect
James Cuthbertson Architects
(incorporating John Boys Architects)

Resident/client profile
Ambulant and non-ambulant with
highly challenging behaviours

DESCRIPTION OF BUILDING

Site context
Urban

Number of resident beds
8

Number of respite or assessment beds
None

Details of other overnight accommodation
Warden maisonette and three guest rooms in adjoining
sheltered housing.

Plan form
No subgroup or clusters

What site constraints or external factors, such as existing buildings or local planning legislation, affected the form and planning of the building?
The surrounding streets are comprised of local authority
maisonettes and terraced housing, well-maintained with
mature planting. The site is adjacent to main thoroughfares.

Construction and external materials
Solid masonry construction with concrete intermediate floors
and tiled pitched roof. Externally two colours of facing brick
with pre-cast concrete details, timber double-glazed windows
and purpose-built conservatory.

Type(s) of flooring
Solid floors to common areas, with non-slip finishes to wet
areas, otherwise carpeted: timber floating floors in flatlets,
apart from wet areas with non-slip vinyl on solid screed laid
to fall.

Internal finishes
Plasterboard dry lining to flats, plasterboard to blockwork to
common areas: plasterboard ceilings to flatlets and suspended
ceilings to corridors.

Equipment
All flatlets have showers; development includes sluice room
and assisted bathroom with Parker bath.

STAFFING

Management staff
32 FTE
Care staff
Day time: 3.25 FTE. Night: 3 x 39 hours.
Other staff
Cleaner 15 hours per week; cook 30 hours per week

(FTE - per week full-time equivalents)

BUILDING STATISTICS

Site area within site boundaries
7,700m²

Ground floor area i.e. 'footprint'
1,700m²

Total floor area
3,200m²

Floor area of individual units of accommodation
25m²

Floor area of common living and dining rooms
50m² (care centre only)

Design for Dementia

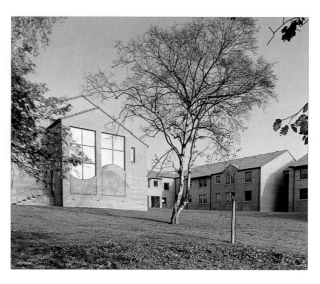

Clockwise from above: Conservatory entrance to the dementia centre; View of gardens enclosed by buildings with the dementia centre on the left; Main entrance to the whole scheme.

Total work costs
£1,822,660

BUILDING DESIGN

The philosophy of care
This was to provide a domestic type of living in a small group and to promote ordinary living – respecting the lives and dignity of the tenants and maintaining their independence of choice at the same time as giving support to carers.

Built expression of design philosophy
Internally, key aspects of the brief included the privacy of the flatlet accommodation, each flatlet with its own shower and WC, the choice of furniture, the provision of a special assisted bathroom and a positive attitude towards the dignity of the residents. For relatives and friends again, privacy of the flatlets was a key consideration as was the provision of a domestic looking building. The staff room has been provided in consideration of the need for staff rest periods and the office is centrally situated within the development.

Other aspects of the building
In the siting of the building care was taken to keep the flatlets back from the busy roads bounding the site and to avoid overlooking, while still maintaining a sense of defensible space, and making the most of the surrounding landscaped areas. The plan of the building responds to the needs for protective internal circulation while at the same time trying to break down long unbroken lengths of corridor and create definable internal space and avoiding monotony or repetition. A key factor has also been to both integrate and provide a separate identity for the care centre within the larger sheltered housing development.

Approach to signage and cueing
Internally there is very little signage in keeping with the attempt to create a domestic appearance. Cueing has been provided for specific tenants within their flatlets.

Approach to colour schemes and interior design
An attempt has been made to provide a sense of calm, with no bold designs or colours, and also to create a homely environment.

Above, the main day area.
Right, the main living space
showing the hearth. Below,
a pleasant outdoor seating area.
Below right, the common
kitchen, looking through the
hatch from the living area.

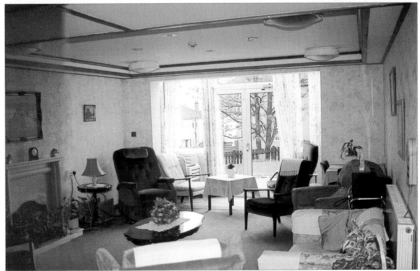

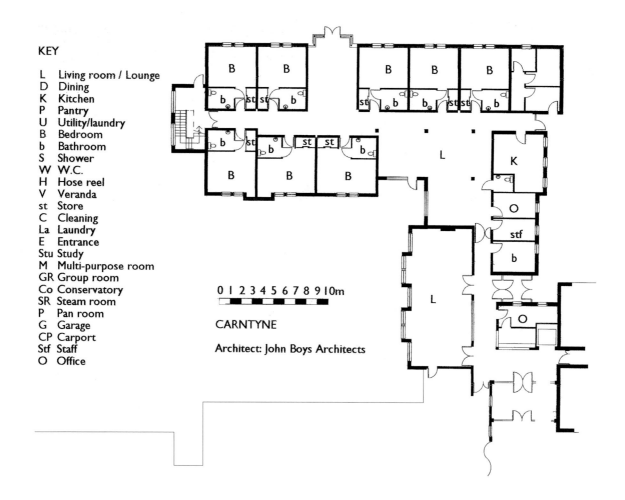

KEY

L   Living room / Lounge
D   Dining
K   Kitchen
P   Pantry
U   Utility/laundry
B   Bedroom
b   Bathroom
S   Shower
W   W.C.
H   Hose reel
V   Veranda
st Store
C   Cleaning
La Laundry
E   Entrance
Stu Study
M   Multi-purpose room
GR Group room
Co Conservatory
SR Steam room
P   Pan room
G   Garage
CP Carport
Stf Staff
O   Office

0 1 2 3 4 5 6 7 8 9 10m

CARNTYNE

Architect: John Boys Architects

Security provisions

These include perimeter fencing, an alarmed door at the rear of the building and, in response to the general open door policy, main doors locked only at dusk.

Heating and/or ventilation system or air conditioning system

Gas-fired central boiler with low surface temperature radiators within flatlets and common areas.

Technology used

This unit is about ordinary daily living – any problems arising from people's dementia will be dealt with very individually, through care plans.

Success in meeting intentions

According to the client the building is certainly being used as intended.

Major hurdles that had to be overcome or prevented the intentions from being achieved

Again, according to the client, none.

Aspects of the building worthy of repetition or to be avoided in future

According to the client, most aspects are worthy of repetition. However, the communal toilet off the main sitting area was not a good idea as people often leave the door open.

Feedback

A summary inspection report from Glasgow City Council Social Work Inspection Unit praised the high standards of physical, social and personal care maintained at Carntyne Gardens. It commented: "Residents demonstrate a strong sense of ownership of their flats which they are free to furnish and decorate as they wish… The communal parts of the home are welcoming and furnished in a style which is familiar and comfortable… Residents consistently speak highly about the quality of life they enjoy and management show a willingness to meet the needs of those accommodated… The Inspector considers that the establishment provides a model of excellence in the provision of resident-centred care."

Bield Housing Association have also had positive feedback from friends and relatives and some staff.

EDITORS' COMMENTS

Carntyne Gardens is a small specialist care housing unit, at the back of a much larger sheltered housing unit. It demonstrates an attempt to design for maximum visual access within the constraints of fire regulations. As a result the bedrooms all open onto a central sitting/dining area; there is a second sitting room area. More seriously the kitchen has had to be a quite separate room. However, an exceptionally large hatch with a steel shutter, almost always open, means that the noise and smells of the kitchen form an important part of the day-to-day activities. Meals are cooked by both staff and residents.

The most satisfying design feature of Carntyne is a cloister effect between the doors of the bedrooms, kitchen and offices; and the central sitting/dining room. The arches provide a degree of separation while barely diminishing the visual access. The sitting/dining room is also given an integrity missing in some of the more barn-like units with high levels of visual access.

The residents' rooms are seen as flatlets, rather than bedrooms in this core housing unit and are often very full of furniture and belongings from past homes. Occasionally low-key additional features, such as a hanging basket, are used to enable residents to find their own front doors.

Impivaarakoti

Reasons for selection

- Eat-in kitchen is focus of house ● More formal dining and lounge area
- Good visual access with (most) bedrooms around living area
- Use of culturally relevant sauna ● Virtually identical to surrounding houses
- Close proximity to shops and transport ● All cooking and laundry on site

Sopimusvuori Foundation — Impivaarakoti
Sukkavartaankatu 9 33100
Tampere
Finland
Tel: + 358 (3) 2141 377
Fax: + 358 (3) 2146 887

Owner
Sopimusvuori Foundation

Contact person for further information
Paivi Karjalainen

Type of building
Nursing home/group home for people with dementia

Architect
Lairto

Resident/client profile
Ambulant and non-ambulant with highly challenging behaviours. A few ambulant, with levels of confusion.

DESCRIPTION OF BUILDING

Site context
The group home, situated within the confines of the city of Tampere, is a small residential estate of detached houses. It is about 5.5 kilometres from the centre of the city.

Number of resident beds
13

Number of respite or assessment beds
None

Details of other overnight accommodation
No overnight accommodation for staff, guest room is in another nursing home nearby.

Plan form
One group

Communal and shared spaces for residents
See floor plan

Staff facilities
Dressing room and toilet

Office and administration space
No separate office and administration space for staff only.

Service and ancillary spaces
See floor plan

What site constraints or external factors, such as existing buildings or local planning legislation, affected the form and planning of the building?
Permitted building volume.
Type of houses in that area.

Construction and external materials
Wooden semi-detached house with a tin roof.

Type(s) of flooring
Most floors are covered with cork but in the living room there is parquet, in the kitchen parquet and marble. In the sauna and bathroom/toilets there is non-slip vinyl floor covering or clinker.

Internal finishes
Cyproc with wallpapers, wooden ceilings, tiled walls in bathrooms/toilets.

Equipment
Special equipment in sauna and in bathroom/toilets (handrails, shower chairs, lowered sauna benches).

Rooms (living rooms) are furnished with beautiful, heavy, old furniture which infirm residents can use for support. This encourages them to walk.

There is no central kitchen – all food is prepared in the common kitchen and residents are encouraged to participate in any daily household chores depending on their abilities and needs. Ordinary kitchen tools are used.

An electric alarm system is provided by each resident's bed.

STAFFING

Management staff
One director
Care staff
Seven staff members
Other staff
Friends and family volunteers, but not on a regular basis.

BUILDING STATISTICS

Site area within site boundaries
1,300m².
Small residential estates comprised of detached houses.

Ground floor area i.e. "footprint"
278m² (6 bedrooms + sitting room + kitchen + sauna department 200m², porch 13m², bedroom with small kitchen 29m² and two bedrooms with small kitchen 36m²)

Total floor area
See above

Design for Dementia

41

A summer party at Impivaarakoti. Note the open door to porch beyond.

Building cost including fixed equipment, hard and soft landscaping (but excluding loose furniture and fittings and professional fees)

2.7 million FIM

BUILDING DESIGN

The philosophy of care

The basic idea at the Sopimusvuori Foundation is to develop all its homes into a therapeutic community. For example residents are encouraged to participate in any daily household chores depending on their abilities and needs, meals are shared and there are no coffee/lunch hours for staff members, no locked offices or other doors except the front door in the winter or the gate door in the summer.

It is important that the homes provide the necessary care for the rest of the residents' life unless special medical care is required. Anxiety, frustration, aggression and depression – the usual symptoms of dementia – are treated with high doses of sedatives in large nursing homes. In our small homes it is possible to focus our attention on every resident as an individual. The therapeutic community gives a safe and secure environment so the usual symptoms rarely occur and the need for sedatives is rather small.

How was the philosophy expressed in the building design?

Internally. For residents: The home looks like other small houses in the same area. "Homelike" living is the main idea and residents have a great deal of freedom. They can walk around the garden, the front door is not locked in summer but the gate door is always locked.

For relatives and friends: Relatives and friends are always welcome. There are no set visiting hours and all homes in the group are well served by public transport.

For staff: The Sopimusvuori Foundation has its own course centre and all staff members are trained in the group's philosophy. It is also important that the group's homes have local contacts in the neighbourhood, with nearby schools etc.

Externally. For residents: There are as few corridors as possible. Most bedrooms open onto the sitting room. Meals are prepared and eaten together. Homelike old furniture is used and there are no locked doors. Living rooms are fully furnished with solid furniture which residents can use for support – thus encouraging them to walk.

Friends and relatives are always welcome to visit and participate in any of the home's activities. It is also possible for them to stay overnight in another nursing home. There are no set visiting hours and support is available.

Siting

The group's homes are situated within the boundaries of the city of Tampere in small residential estates comprised of detached houses. They are about 5.5 kilometres from the centre of the city.

Plan form

The plan has bedrooms around the living room opening directly onto it. The kitchen is placed between the entrance hall and the living room. One room and two apartments have been added to the original building.

External character and appearance

The home looks like any other small house in the same area.

Approach and entrance

The building is designed to look like a home and blend in with its surroundings.

Approach to signage and cueing

Most of the bedrooms open onto the sitting room. Residents' first names are displayed in block letters at the doors to their bedrooms. The sitting rooms and dining room are open spaces and easy to find.

Approach to colour schemes and interior design

Special attention has been paid to ensuring that the home is light and clear and as home-like as possible. Windows have been placed so that residents can see out when sitting.

Security provisions

A special electrical alarm system under the floors in front of beds is in all the group's new homes and is also planned for Impivaarakoti.

Heating and/or ventilation system or air conditioning system

District heating. An air-conditioning system stores up the heat.

Technology used

Electrical wooden beds and a special alarm system under the floor in front of beds.

Success in meeting intentions

The intentions were met in all respects.

Major hurdles that had to be overcome or prevented the intentions from being achieved

Money.

Above, using the terrace in summer. Below, a religious service in the living room.

Aspects of the building design worthy of replication?
At present the group is building two new homes, using the information gained from the existing eight homes (the first founded in 1991) and also the information from the research mentioned above.

To be avoided in the future?
No more single rooms. Old people have lived most of their lives with other people and shared their bedrooms with hus-band or wife. They feel safer when they can hear someone's breathing near by.

Feedback
STAKES (National Research and Development Centre for Welfare and Health) and Sopimusvuori Foundation have stud-ied the ground plan effect on the quality and also on the cost of the care. This research studied 12 different units, both from

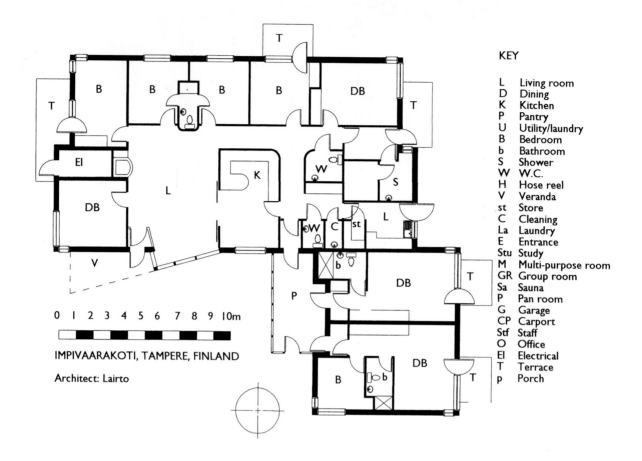

KEY

L   Living room
D   Dining
K   Kitchen
P   Pantry
U   Utility/laundry
B   Bedroom
b   Bathroom
S   Shower
W   W.C.
H   Hose reel
V   Veranda
st Store
C   Cleaning
La Laundry
E   Entrance
Stu Study
M   Multi-purpose room
GR Group room
Sa Sauna
P   Pan room
G   Garage
CP Carport
Stf Staff
O   Office
El Electrical
T   Terrace
p   Porch

IMPIVAARAKOTI, TAMPERE, FINLAND

Architect: Lairto

traditional big nursing homes and from small group homes and the aim was to encourage the politicians and the staff members to give attention to how much the environment affects, and also improves, the quality of the care. The staff of those 12 units were interviewed and 38 residents were observed in this research. This information was used in the plan form of these two new group homes.

EDITORS' COMMENT

Impivaarakoti is a very pleasant traditional Finnish timber one-storey house, in a wooded suburb of Tampere, surrounded by similar houses, all in their own private gardens. There is another home adjoining which allows sharing of night staff. Of the nine bedrooms only four are singles, a result of feedback from residents who in many cases prefer to share.

The porch provides a pleasant entrance and allows provision for outdoor clothes and footwear – very necessary in the Finnish climate. Six bedrooms, two doubles and two singles, appear to be part of the original house with the remaining rooms being part of an extension linked by the porch.

The original six bedrooms open off the living room or a short corridor leading off it which with the centrally-placed kitchen produces a compact plan with good visual connections between the spaces. The remaining three rooms are removed from the living space and kitchen and are adaptations of a self-contained bedsitting room and a one-bedroom flat. This may be the result of Scandinavian interest in maintaining flexibility for the future.

The living room has an angled bay window and a door which opens on to a covered terrace. It overlooks the main garden area, the front door and the road beyond giving a strong visual link to the outside world. It is domestic in scale and full of furniture in the way that real "homes" often are.

The very central, visually accessible position of the kitchen, which it is natural to use as part of the circulation space, works

to create a truly domestic, family and non institutional atmosphere. En suite facilities only exist for two bedrooms which share one shower room and a washbasin is only provided in one other room. WCs are not visually accessible and are located some way, up to 11 metres, from bedroom doors.

Impivaarakoti is a near-perfect example of how a building designed for dementia care can be virtually identical to the other houses which it adjoins; there is nothing which sets it apart from its neighbours as being in any way special. It is of similar size, built of similar materials and occupies a plot of similar area to the other houses along the road. Inside, the furniture, fittings and finishes are those of a typical Finnish or Scandinavian home, timber parquet floors, rugs hanging on the walls and of course the traditional stove in the living room.

The care management is positively participatory, the impression is one of a large, but close-knit, family. It is an important reminder that good design for dementia care is not merely a case of satisfying a series of abstract rules but of the need to understand the fundamental principles of what constitutes "home", something which transcends function. It is important, however, to note that it does not exist in isolation, sharing night staff with a similar house on the opposite side of the road.

Parkside Court

Reasons for selection

- Re-modelled facility — had to retain heritage building • Extensive use of redundant cueing • Use of natural light • Free access to external areas • Blends in with surrounding neighbourhoods • Good sized bedrooms with "olde worlde" feel

Parkside Court
53 Parkside Street
Elsternwick VIC 3185
Australia
Tel: (+61) 3 9818 0998
Fax: (+61) 3 9818 0911

Owner
Anglican Homes for the Elderly

Contact person for further information
Mrs Imas Thompson, Executive Director
Anglican Homes for the Elderly
83 Riversdale Road,
Hawthorn VIC 3122

Type of building
Hostel/residential home

Architect
Kerr, Lewit, Clark and Kidd
68 Oxford Street
Collingwood VIC 3066
Tel: (+61) 3 9419 0299
Contact: Ms Kirsty Bennett

Resident/client profile
Ambulant with highly challenging behaviours and levels of confusion

DESCRIPTION OF BUILDING

Site context
Suburban

Number of resident beds
13

Number of respite or assessment beds
None

Details of other overnight accommodation
No staff bedroom or guest rooms, However fold-up beds can be arranged for relatives to stay over if necessary. A self-contained unit above the hostel (part of the building) is let to a staff member who can be called upon in an emergency.

Plan form
Two clusters (one of seven residents and one of six residents).

Communal and shared spaces for residents
Unit 1. Kitchen, dining and lounge rooms, one additional toilet near living areas, spa bath (internal) – room also has shower and toilet.
Unit 2. Kitchen, dining and lounge rooms, two bedrooms each for two residents plus two single bedrooms, two shared showers and toilets and one room with bath, shower and toilet.

Staff facilities
Designed with staff base area now utilised for other purposes – staff use adjacent hostel facilities.

Office and administration space
No separate office and administration in the unit. Office space is in the co-located hostel.

Service and ancillary spaces
Two domestic-scale kitchens (main kitchen in co-located hostel); domestic-style laundry for cleaning residents' personal items including a sluice facility; shared linen store, six en suite facilities and four shared en suite bathrooms.

What site constraints or external factors, such as existing buildings or local planning legislation, affected the form and planning of the building?
Co-located with existing hostel building. Limited land space available. Existing Edwardian home was required to be retained. Had to fit into suburban streetscape.

Construction and external materials
Mixture of solid brick and brick veneer construction, concrete slab floor to extensions to existing house roof. Tile or slate to match existing.

Type(s) of flooring
Living areas (lounge and dining rooms), bedrooms, passageways and non-service areas are carpeted.
Bathrooms and en suites have non-slip vinyl with covered skirting. Kitchens and laundry have slip-resistant vinyl.
Floor tiles are used in the link between the units.

Internal finishes
Generally finishes are plasterboard and paint (domestic in nature). Existing building has internal brick walls with decorative solid plastering.

Equipment
All bathrooms are fitted for older people.

STAFFING

Management staff
One full-time manager for the total complex – 50 per cent of time allocated to this unit. Deputy manager/registered nurse – 5 hours per week.

Care staff
Rostered 24 hours, including overnight (overnight staff shared with co-located hostel). Full time equivalent – 5.0 per week.

Other staff
Administrative staff – 10 hours per week. Co-ordinator of Volunteers – 10 hours per week. Maintenance staff – 10 hours per week. Food/Domestic staff – appointed time per week 15 hours.

BUILDING STATISTICS

Site area within site boundaries
2,821m²

Ground floor area i.e. "footprint"
571.7m²

Total floor area
631.7m²

Floor area of individual units of accommodation
Range from 17m² to 21m²

Floor area of common living and dining rooms per group or cluster as appropriate (excluding separate circulation space and corridors)
Lounges approximately 20m²
Kitchen and dining rooms approximately 25m².

Building cost including fixed equipment, hard and soft landscaping (but excluding loose furniture and fittings and professional fees)
A$841,291

BUILDING DESIGN

The philosophy of care
The philosophy of care and the approaches used at Parkside Court Dementia Unit are based on the benefits of holistic care

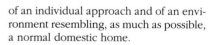

Above, a resident's personal space in the renovated annexe. Right, the link between the old and the new units. Below, kitchen/dining area with window overlooking front door and street. Opposite page, Parkside Court's front entrance.

of an individual approach and of an environment resembling, as much as possible, a normal domestic home.

Residents are perceived as having individual needs, as having strengths as well as support needs.

The units offer a flexible programme of a homelike and domestic nature which allows and encourages each resident to maintain personal optimal daily living and social skills. This is achieved by:

- Enabling the residents to participate in the daily operation of the unit so that it reflects, as far as possible, a typical suburban residence.
- Enabling residents to maintain and/or develop their own identity by having access to a normal set of choices.
- Encouraging family and friends to stay involved with residents as an integral part of the residents' support.
- Maintaining strong and regular links with residents and the community.

How was the philosophy expressed in the design of the building?

Internally.

For residents: The building design reflects a "normal" domestic environment. Small kitchens, lounge areas, dining areas and bedrooms are located close together. There are no long corridors or passageways. The units are decorated and furnished to look like an average home. Residents can find their way around and become familiar with the small buildings. Residents can be supported to participate in using the kitchen area, etc.

For relatives: As well as the measures above, families like to see the small, homelike environment and see their relative settle and feel comfortable in their home. Families use the domestic lounge or dining area when visiting. Families also feel comfortable as the unit is less imposing then a larger building/hostel. Families are encouraged to visit whenever they are able – there are no set visiting times.

For staff: The small domestic environment assists staff to understand that this is really the residents' home. The kitchen is user-friendly, the unit looks inviting and easy to manage.

Externally.

For residents: There is a large garden and walking area where residents who are restless can wander. The external doors are not locked during daylight hours and residents can access the garden without feeling that they are "locked in". The secure perimeter fence ensures that residents are unable to leave the grounds. The building looks like the rest of the neighbourhood and perhaps does not stigmatise residents as much as a named/labelled hostel would.

For relatives and friends: As well as the above, families often use the pleasant garden area.

For staff: Staff feel happy that residents can wander safely but know that they are secure. Staff also enjoy the fact that the units look like the surrounding neighbourhood.

Siting

Parkside Court is built on a rectangular site of 2,821m² which is bounded to the south by Clarence Street and to the east by Parkside Street. An existing hostel and Edwardian house, (known as the Annexe) were located on the western part of the site prior to its construction.

Parkside Court consists of extensions to this Annexe, the erection of a new adjoining six-person unit, a link which connects these buildings to the existing hostel and separates them from each other.

The two units have been sited to create a clearly identifiable street address with clear separation from the existing hostel building, thereby emphasising the residential nature of the units and their place as part of the local community, rather than part of a larger complex of buildings.

An non-palisade fence defines the Parkside and Clarence Street boundaries. Front gates to each of the houses are set back from the street and planting was designed to divide the front yard into two areas. A courtyard has been created between the two houses to separate the units and provide a sheltered area for sitting and gardening.

Plan form

Parkside Court consists of two separate houses, the Annexe which has been renovated and extended to accommodate seven residents, and a new purpose-built unit for six people.

Extensions to the Annexe consist of a kitchen and dining area and a single bedroom. The bathroom area has been renovated, a lounge room created in an existing bedroom and a new staircase built to serve the upstairs attic. En suite and bathroom facilitates are located centrally and shared by residents. These are readily accessed from bedrooms and require minimum travel. The Annexe has been planned to allow residents to move through the building continuously if they wish to. Corridors are minimised and end at social spaces, thereby drawing residents back to the "heart" or "hub" of the building

where staff and other residents can generally be found.

In contrast the new unit is designed as a linear building with social spaces facing the street. A corridor leads from these areas past the six bedrooms and terminates at the link with Annexe and co-located hostel.

The buildings are connected by a discreet link which is set back from the street. The link is of lightweight construction of timber and glass with a tiled floor to provide a sense of an indoor/outdoor space and to make it clear that a person is leaving their residential unit.

External character and appearance

Parkside has been designed to respond to the surrounding neighbourhood which has a strong residential character and high quality building stock. The presence of the Annexe on the site gave a clear context for the units. Extensions to the Annexe continued finishes which were used in this building where possible, for example through the use of a slate roof, while the new unit used appropriate yet more contemporary material such as terracotta tiles.

Landscaping and paving were designed to complement the layout of the building, directing residents back to the entrances, lounge and dining areas. Plants were selected to provide visual and olfactory cues, for example by placing lavender below bedroom windows on the north side of the new unit.

Approach and entrance

Parkside Court is approached from Parkside Street through front gates placed before paths which lead directly to the front door of each unit.

Approach to signage and cueing

Minimal signage has been used in the building. Cueing techniques such as natural lighting, changes in wall and floor textures, colours, identifiable architectural details, recognisable and distinctive individual room designs have been used to positively compensate for residents' sensory and memory losses.

The placement of bedroom doors and windows has been varied to emphasise the individual nature of each and every room. A minimum of fixed furniture was provided to leave residents the freedom to personalise their own spaces.

Approach to colour schemes and interior design

Colours have been used at Parkside Court to give rooms a recognisable identity and to provide a cue for residents. Themes have been taken from the colours of windows and decorative tiles in the Annexe and have been selected as being age-appropriate. Wall colours are generally more restrained, with accent colours being used on architraves, skirting and picture rails.

Furniture has been selected to be familiar and welcoming. Seat height, cushion design, etc. have been modified to suit resident needs and provide assistance, as well as comfort.

Security provisions

Access and egress from the site is restricted by the fence and gates. Movement from and within the buildings is not restricted during the day, although kitchens have been located so that staff can surreptitiously obscure entry points. If necessary kitchen and dining rooms can be closed off.

Heating and/or ventilation system or air conditioning system

Hydronic heating is provided to all rooms. Social spaces are cooled with a reverse cycle air-conditioner.

Technology used

Keypads have been installed on front gates to control movement from the site.

Success in meeting intentions

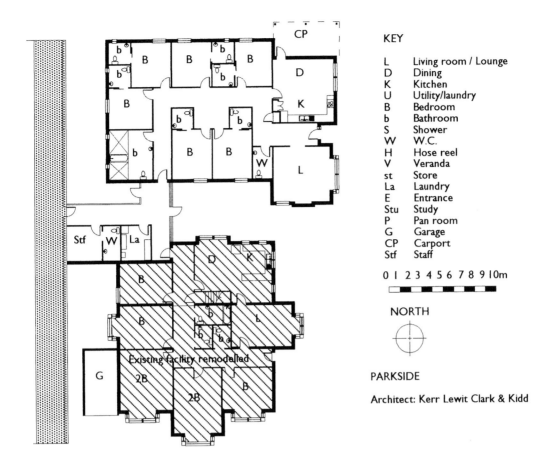

Parkside Court is a small-scale residential building which affirms the dignity of residents and forms part of the local community. As such it has achieved its design goals.

Major hurdles that had to be overcome or prevented the intentions from being achieved

The incorporation of the Annexe presented a challenge which has been successfully met, providing an example of successful renovation of an existing building to create a purpose designed environment for people with dementia.

Aspects of the building design worthy of replication?

- Small domestic style
- Free access to outside areas
- Individual rooms with en suites
- Secure garden freely accessible to residents
- Street relationship and community links

To be avoided in the future?

- Small size makes financial viability difficult.
- Individual mouldings on doors to enable residents' identification do not work.
- Gas log fires, which provide no real heat, confuse residents.

Feedback

People with dementia seem to settle into the building and find its domestic style and size familiar.

Families and friends like the building because of its domestic and homelike design. Families prefer the single rooms.

Staff find the design easy to work in although, at times when only one staff member is on duty, supervision is difficult because of the separate nature of the units.

EDITORS' COMMENT

Most of the Australian examples in this book are purpose-designed environments for people with dementia. However, most care providers are confronted with the difficulty of remodelling existing buildings to accommodate dementia residents. Parkside Court is the only (Australian) example in this book which has successfully integrated good dementia design into an existing building with a limited budget, although there are others, including Banksia at Wesley Gardens and Woodberry Village, both in the suburbs of Sydney.

Parkside Court has used the existing buildings to advantage so that the high ceilings and generous bedrooms give ample individual spaces. The homeliness of Parkside Court has been enhanced by the bedroom furniture and fittings while, from the street, the building blends in superbly with the surrounding neighbourhood.

Effort has been made to employ as much redundant cueing as possible. This has been in the form of natural lighting, changes in wall and floor textures, colours, identifiable architectural details and recognisable and distinctive individual room designs. Bedroom doors and windows have been uniquely placed to emphasise the individual nature of each room.

Lindern

- *Re-modelled 1920's building on urban site* • *Multi-level for ambulant and non-ambulant* • *Communal areas in centre of each floor* • *Excellent natural light in communal areas* • *Large bedrooms* • *All cooking and laundry on each floor.*
- *Good visibility of surrounding parks and buildings.*

Lindern eldrekollektiv,
Stensgata 43
0454 Oslo
Norway
Tel: (+47) 22 56 89 81

Owner
The Municipality of Oslo,
District of St Hanshaugan and Ulleväl
Pilestredet 75
0453 Oslo

Managing organisation
PRO-base
Kirkevn 161
0450 Oslo
Tel: (+47) 22 69 66 50

Contact person for further information
Urszula Østby, manager at Lindern eldrekollektiv

Type of building
Residential home with expertise in dementia on the first and second floors. On the ground floor and basement there is a day centre, which receives six to eight clients seven days a week during the daytime (8.30am until 2pm when dinner is served) and six clients in the afternoons five days a week (2-8pm). This service started in July 1997.

Treatment rooms and offices for the district's physiotherapy and occupational therapy services occupy the building's attic, but are independent of the home.

Architect
Lien & Fossland, Architects MNAL, Oslo

Lindern: A view of the living room with a corridor beyond.

Above, outside view from Stensgata showing the curved appearance. Below, the garden in winter.

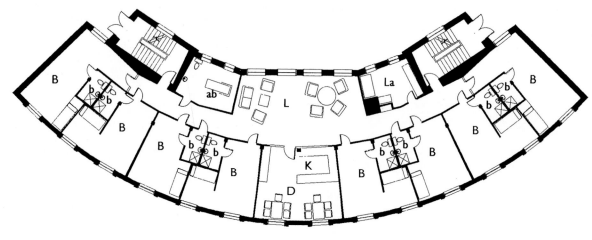

KEY

L	Living room / Lounge	Stu	Study
D	Dining	M	Multi-purpose room
K	Kitchen	GR	Group room
P	Pantry	Co	Conservatory
U	Utility/laundry	SR	Steam room
B	Bedroom	P	Pan room
b	Bathroom	G	Garage
ab	Assisted bath	CP	Carport
S	Shower	Stf	Staff
W	W.C.	O	Office
H	Hose reel		
V	Veranda		
st	Store		
C	Cleaning		
La	Laundry		
E	Entrance		

0 1 2 3 4 5 6 7 8 9 10m

LINDERN, OSLO

Architect: Lien og Fossland

Resident/client profile
Ambulant, with levels of confusion and different types of dementia problems.

DESCRIPTION OF BUILDING

Site context
Urban

Number of resident beds
15. (Seven on the first floor and eight on the second).

Number of respite/assessment beds or other overnight accommodation
One respite/assessment bed. There is no other overnight accommodation.

Communal and shared spaces for residents
First floor – sitting room, kitchen and laundry.
Second floor – sitting room, kitchen, laundry, bathroom and sluice room.

Staff facilities
Smoking room in the basement by the day centre.

Office and administration space
Two offices, one for the manager and one for the staff.

Service and ancillary spaces
One laundry in the basement, where there is also a room for the heating system and offices for the caretakers in the district.

What site constraints or external factors, such as existing buildings or local planning legislation, affected the form and planning of the building?
The house was built about 1900 and used to have smaller apartments (cabins) for single women who worked as maids for the wealthy people in this district. The house was rebuilt in 1986 and opened as a residential home in 1987. The shape of the house follows the street and the crossroads and forms a light curve. This makes the house easily recognisable. The neighbourhood has the same type of houses, but smaller. All houses are surrounded by gardens.

Construction and external materials
Bricks and concrete outside.

Type(s) of flooring
Linoleum on first and second floors. Tiles in the day centre.

Internal finishes
Walls are concrete and wood (plates). The ceiling is concrete covered with special ceiling plates.

Equipment
A bath tub which can be elevated, rails in the bathrooms by the showers and toilets. There is a seat on the wall by the shower.

STAFFING

Management staff
One manager (37.5 hrs/per week)

Care staff

16.5 positions for care staff (three of these work in the day centre).

Other staff

0.5 positions for a cleaning assistant. A general practitioner is in attendance 2.5 hours a week and more if needed.

BUILDING STATISTICS

Ground floor area i.e. "footprint"

Ground floor	200m²
1st floor	400m²
2nd floor	400m²
Attic	400m²

Total floor area

1400m²

Floor area of individual units of accommodation

From 21.2 to 25.2m² (on first and second floors only)

Floor area of common living and dining rooms per group or cluster as appropriate (excluding separate circulation space and corridors)

106.5m²

Building cost including fixed equipment, hard and soft landscaping (but excluding loose furniture and fittings and professional fees)

Rebuilding cost was estimated as 5,278,100 Norwegian kroner in 1986.

BUILDING DESIGN

The philosophy of care

That the residents will increase or maintain their level of function as long as possible by participating in all kinds of activities that a normal day demands.

To live at Lindern eldrekollektiv shall be as similar as possible to living in one's own home.

How was the philosophy expressed in the design of the building?

Residents can participate in all kinds of activities, such as making dinner, baking cakes, ironing, cleaning their rooms or gardening, if they enjoy them. The feeling of doing something useful restores the residents' self-esteem and self-respect, which has often been lost because of the losses the disease creates.

Relatives and friends know that the resident has become a member of a large family. The building has been designed so that staff are always available. They cannot go and hide in other rooms. The philosophy is that, for both residents and staff, being together is most important.

Siting

The building is situated at a road junction within walking distance of the centre of Oslo.

Plan form

Lightly curved building with kitchen and sitting room in the middle. This keeps the corridors short and the residents always have a view over the area, which makes them feel safe.

There are four residential rooms on each side of the communal space.

External character and appearance

The curving form of the building and its proportions are attractive and similar in character to adjoining residential buildings.

Approach and entrance

There are two entrances, one on each side. There are stairs with about seven steps, with rails on each side.

Approach to signage and cueing

The front of the stairs is marked with yellow tape. All resident's doors are marked with their names and there is a little lamp outside each door. The doors have mailboxes for the resident's paper, mail, etc.

Approach to colour schemes and interior design

There are different colours on each floor and different colours for the furniture. Most of the furniture has been inherited.

Security provisions

The doors are locked and the doors have door bells for each floor. The building is looked after by a Securitas night patrol and has a direct line to the fire department. Sometimes the kitchen doors have to be locked.

Heating and/or ventilation system or air conditioning system

Central heating (radiators).

Technology used

There is a bell by each bed, but the residents often forget to use them. The building is not very insulated so the staff can hear if something is wrong. There is no other technology.

Success in meeting intentions

The building is very well suited to its purpose.

Major hurdles that had to be overcome or prevented the intentions from being achieved

None known

Aspects of the building design worthy of replication?

The curved shape; communal rooms in the middle of the unit; short corridors; homely atmosphere. Glass windows between the kitchen and the sitting room create a great view and provide safety and tranquillity.

To be avoided in the future?

Thresholds and narrow doors into the bathrooms. One could also wish for a larger laundry with possibilities to hang and dry clothes, and a balcony and veranda to enjoy outdoor air in a sheltered space.

Feedback

Everyone has been very positive.

EDITORS' COMMENTS

Lindern is a converted former hostel building located in a pleasant residential inner suburb of Oslo within easy walking distance of the town centre. Its gently curving plan results from the corner site.

The semi-basement of the three-storey building is used for a day centre and ancillary accommodation including workshop and storage areas. The first and second floors are nearly identical and provide a self-contained residential cluster for seven or eight people each. The attic is used for a therapy centre, totally independent of the two residential floors.

The building has staircases at both ends of a central corridor (there is no lift) and was originally planned with bedrooms continuously along both sides. The conversion has been carried out by removing partition walls between bedrooms and a wall on one side of the corridor at the midway point between the two staircases. This has created a living room in the centre of the plan with a kitchen on the other side, separated from the living room by a glazed screen.

All food is prepared in the kitchen which is open to the dining room and used by residents. All meals are taken at restau-

Above, view of the living room with door and window to kitchen on right. Below, the dining room.

Above, the kitchen is open to the dining room and used by residents. Below, a typical resident's bedroom.

One of Lindern's residents working in the kitchen.

rant type tables and there is no provision for more informal eating.

The individual rooms are generous in area, 21.2 – 25.2m² and the short length of corridor extending a little way on either side of the centrally placed living room and kitchen provides good visual access into the living room from outside bedroom doors. At the same time it prevents views from one end of the building to the other and so creates a small-scale, domestic, non-institutional character.

The gently curved plan form recurs at Moorside, a new building in Winchester, UK, with similar happy results except that national fire regulations make it necessary to close off both living and dining rooms with glazed doors and screens, so generating a more institutional character.

This plan form appears to work well. It is efficient, in space utilisation and cost terms, with bedrooms "double banked" along the central corridor, so keeping circulation space to a minimum and, as demonstrated at Lindern, permitting the building to be used in different ways during the useful life of the structure.

The building is simple and elegant externally, if slightly forbidding in the absence of any entrance doors or connections to the outside world which are visible from the road. The absence of a lift and of direct connections to the outside and the restricted site area (there is only a small terrace at ground level) are less than ideal. However, in its location and internal character, Lindern works very well, although the generous living area has more of the character of a hotel lounge than of a domestic living room.

Design for Dementia

Riverview Lodge

Reasons for selection

● *Important historic place in dementia design thinking* ● *Small behaviour management units* ● *Good visual access* ● *Simple garden area for walking, sitting, gardening* ● *Health service unit.*

Riverview Lodge
The Confused and Disturbed Elderly Unit (CADE)
Bungay Road
Wingham NSW 2429
Australia
Tel: (+61) 2 6557 0562
Fax: (+61) 2 6557 0183

Owner and managing organisation
Mid North Coast Health Service
Southern Sector
PO Box 35
Taree NSW 2430
Tel: (+61) 2 6551 1293

Contact person for further information
Ruth Greentree
Nurse Unit Manager
Riverview Lodge
Bungay Road
Wingham NSW 2429
Australia
Tel: (+61) 2 6557 0562
or
Del Heuke
Clinical Nurse Consultant
Aged and Extended Care
Bungay Road
Wingham NSW 2429
Australia
Tel: (+61) 2 6557 0555

Type of building
Group home, long term accommodation facility for the confused and disturbed elderly. One room is reserved for short term, assessment purposes.

Architect
P. A. O'Neill Partners Pty Ltd

Resident/client profile
Ambulant, with highly challenging behaviours and levels of confusion

DESCRIPTION OF BUILDING

Site context
Riverview Lodge is situated on the Wingham Hospital grounds located in a suburban area. The unit is located in suburbia so that the residents will at least have the opportunity to observe everyday life and whenever possible to take part in it.

Number of resident beds
15

Number of respite or assessment beds
One

Details of other overnight accommodation
No other designated rooms. However, short term accommodation could be provided for a limited number of residents' relatives.

Plan form
The unit is divided into two mirror-imaged sides separated by staff and administrative areas. Each side accommodates eight residents.

Communal and shared spaces for residents
● Dining room: The dining room is an open-planned area directly behind the kitchen. There is immediate access from the kitchen and the furniture comprises two sets of tables and chairs. The residents use this area for all meals.
● Lounge room: The largest section within the unit is the lounge room furnished with two-seater sofas and numerous armchairs. This area is considered to be a resting place for the residents and there is a large television set for them to watch. There is access to the sunroom and to an outdoor area from the lounge room.
● Bathroom: Situated off the dining room, the bathroom is fully tiled with a toilet and washbasin. The bathroom is spacious allowing adequate space for staff to assist residents. A locked cupboard stores towels, toiletries, etc.
● Showers: Two showers are situated off the lounge room. These showers are fully tiled. A toilet and double basin vanity unit with a large mirror is also incorporated into each shower unit.
● Toilet: There are four toilets for communal use. Each toilet is generously sized. One toilet is located outside for ease of access when residents are in the garden.
● Sunroom: Adjacent to the lounge room the sunroom is a quiet place where residents can enjoy an outlook over the gardens. Comfortable seating is provided in the area.
● Outdoor areas: The unit has generous, beautifully-landscaped gardens surrounded by secure perimeter fencing. Both sheltered seating and garden seats are provided for the use of residents and their visitors. A barbecue area also provides a popular eating venue in summer.

Design for Dementia

Due to the lie of the land it was impossible to capitalise on spectacular views over the Manning River.

Staff facilities

The nurses' station is the central location between the two resident areas. Access from the residents' quarters are through locked doors from both kitchens. This room is a multipurpose area where educational meetings, shift handovers and resident reviews are attended. The nurses also use it for meal breaks.

The staff have access to staff-only toilet and shower facilities which also are fully tiled. Staff lockers and notice board are located in a separate room adjacent to the nurses' station.

Office and administration space

The nursing unit manager has an office close to the main entrance to the unit.

Service and ancillary spaces

Kitchen: The kitchen is approximately proportioned the same as a normal home with an outlook onto the garden. Residents assist with meal preparation and cleaning. A safety door is inconspicuously incorporated into the bench design to allow staff to limit access to the kitchen if required.

Laundry: Residents are encouraged to assist staff with the laundering of personal effects. Residents hang their clothes on a Rotar's Clothesline, similar to the facilities most people have in their own homes.

Treatment room: This is a double-locked room where medication and treatment supplies are stored.

What site constraints or external factors, such as existing buildings or local planning legislation, affected the form and planning of the building?

The unit was built on the established grounds of Wingham Hospital. Unfortunately, due to the lie of the land the architect was unable to capitalise on the beautiful view afforded of the Manning River.

Construction and external materials

The unit is of double brick construction on a concrete slab. A timber frame structure was utilised. A green colour bond roof assists to blend the building structure into the environment.

Type(s) of flooring

The unit is fully carpeted except for the kitchen, dining room and bedroom areas where vinyl sheet flooring is laid. Bathroom and shower facilities are fully tiled.

Internal finishes

The walls are constructed of Cyproc with a washable, painted finish in soft colours.

Equipment

Hand grips are provided in shower and bathroom areas.

STAFFING

Management staff

One nurse manager	1.0 FTE
One program manager	0.5 FTE

Care staff

Seven registered nurses	4.4 FTE
Six enrolled nurses	6.0 FTE
Five assistants in nursing	4.35 FTE

Other staff

Cleaner grade one	0.2 FTE

BUILDING STATISTICS

Ground floor area i.e. "footprint"

790.6m²

Above, an open-plan design for the central living area with total visual access. Below, access to the kitchen is through an inconspicuous opening in the bench design. Next to the kitchen a door opens onto an outside patio and there is a locked door that leads from the kitchen to the nurses' station.

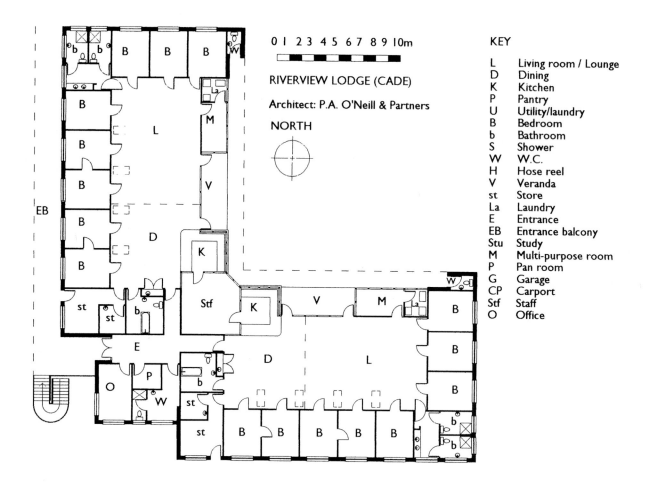

0 1 2 3 4 5 6 7 8 9 10m

RIVERVIEW LODGE (CADE)

Architect: P.A. O'Neill & Partners

NORTH

KEY

L	Living room / Lounge
D	Dining
K	Kitchen
P	Pantry
U	Utility/laundry
B	Bedroom
b	Bathroom
S	Shower
W	W.C.
H	Hose reel
V	Veranda
st	Store
La	Laundry
E	Entrance
EB	Entrance balcony
Stu	Study
M	Multi-purpose room
P	Pan room
G	Garage
CP	Carport
Stf	Staff
O	Office

Total floor area
1,030.8m²

Floor area of individual units of accommodation
10.5m²

Floor area of common living and dining rooms per group or cluster as appropriate (excluding separate circulation space and corridors)
111.9m²

Building cost including fixed equipment, hard and soft landscaping (but excluding loose furniture and fittings and professional fees)
A$903,252

BUILDING DESIGN

The philosophy of care

Riverview Lodge offers specialised residential care for the confused and disturbed elderly in a simple, safe, environment that encourages a feeling of security and familiarity.

We see residents as being elderly people with a particular disability, that of dementia, who should be treated with the patience and courtesy normally extended to respected elders.

We endeavour to provide a warm, secure, stable environment, in which the dementing person can participate in familiar activities and feel at home.

Any restrictions on wandering are kept as unobtrusive as possible with staff spending time with residents, talking to them slowly, clearly and simply, prompting and assisting them throughout the normal activities of daily living. We are prepared to discover resident's interests, background, likes and dislikes, to be able to relate to residents and their families as supportive carers. We do allow them the dignity of risk.

In keeping with the philosophy of care, residents are allowed to enjoy the dignity of taking the normal risks associated with usual day to day activities.

How was the philosophy expressed in the design of the building?

Internally. Provision of a homelike environment for residents was the underpinning of the building design. An open planned area was created for the main living areas. This provides residents with a simple, uncluttered environment that promotes familiarity. The colour scheme was carefully chosen to provide a calm atmosphere. Security aspects of the building and grounds are unobtrusive but maximise resident security and dignity.

The studies regarding the number of residents that should live together in a dementia unit were taken into consideration. Based on these studies eight residents are housed on either side of the unit with separate grounds and living space for each area. Each resident has their own bedroom affording them personal dignity and space. Although the unit has modern facilities the soft furnishings reflect the era of the residents.

Relatives and friends are welcome at the unit and are encouraged to continue with resident contact. Provision of sitting areas in the lounge room, sunroom and garden allows personal visits. Car parking, with disabled access, is provided for relatives and friends.

Even though a homelike environment is provided the staff are able to view residents from all living areas. Adequate space is provided in bathroom areas to allow staff to perform assistant duties.

A security system alerts staff when residents are out of bed and there is a concern for resident safety. The location of the nurses' station is designed to enable immediate access to resident areas. The nurses' station also provides a discrete area for staff access only.

Externally. The grounds are reasonably flat with easy access from the dining room and sunroom. The paved barbecue area provides shelter in all weather. Garden seats allow the residents to enjoy the outdoor surrounds. The residents can wander freely due to the secure perimeter fencing. Relatives and friends have access to the outdoor areas with the residents.

The open-planned design allows staff to view the residents when they are in the garden from other areas of the garden or from the main living areas.

Siting
Riverview Lodge was constructed as an adjunct to the services provided at Wingham Hospital. Although physically separated from Wingham Hospital, the site was chosen to maximise interaction between the two units. For example, wandering patients can be cared for during the day at Riverview Lodge.

Riverview Lodge was built by the Aged Community Service, and together with the rehabilitation services of Wingham Hospital, provides comprehensive aged care.

Plan Form
The plan was based on the brief given to the architect regarding designing a building combining residents' needs, aged care services and the available site.

External character and appearance
The building was designed to be as unobtrusive as possible on the surrounds. The colours blend well with the rural outlook.

Approach and entrance
There is one external entry point to the unit which provides extra security. There are no steps to the entry with a flat path to the main door. A hand rail is provided to assist relatives or friends along the path. The entry point to the unit is via a locked door and opens into a reception area.

Approach to signage and cueing
Adequate signage is provided to the unit for relatives and friends.

Approach to colour schemes and interior design
The furniture, ornaments, and paintings are of the era recognised by the residents. The "type" of soft furnishings usually seen in their previous homes. The colour scheme is soft with colours blending together to provide a calm, restful atmosphere.

Security provisions
Security provisions include a safety fence surrounding the entire perimeter at the back of the unit. A safety fence divides the unit into two sections allowing eight residents on both sides to have their own yard area.

The unit has two exit doors which are locked and the entrance door to the unit is also locked. Staff are provided with keys to all areas.

Heating and/or ventilation system or air conditioning system
The unit has ceiling fans, for the summer months. During winter, two centrally located heaters are mounted on the walls and small heaters are located in each of the residents' rooms.

Technology used
As the residents are cared for in an environment as homelike as possible technology is kept to a minimum. The only technology currently in use is bed alarms alerting staff when resi-

Doors to bedrooms open off the central living and dining area.

The garden is designed for easy maintenance. The safety perimeter fencing is unobtrusive and blends into the surroundings. (Note the external WC — the famous Australian "dunny".)

dents leave their bed during the night. These alarms are utilised with new admissions being assessed and residents who wander or are at risk of falling.

Various assessment programmes and management plans are utilised to achieve the best possible outcomes for the residents. Programmes are built into everyday, needs-based activities that emphasise independent functioning.

An Revised Elderly Persons Disability Scale (REPDS) assessment plan is implemented pre-admission, one week after admission, monthly and at four-monthly intervals to monitor changes over time.

Success in meeting intentions
The building is extremely well designed for the care of dementia patients.

Major hurdles that had to be overcome or prevented the intentions from being achieved
No major problems have been reported. An excellent result was obviously achieved.

Aspects of the building design worthy of replication
This unit is ideal for the care of dementia patients. There is a need for this building design to be incorporated into the development of nursing homes.

Feedback
Positive verbal feedback has been obtained from some residents. However the level of dementia of the majority of residents is such that qualitative feedback is impossible.

The friends and relatives constantly inform the staff of their appreciation of the high standard of care and the emphasis placed on retaining a homelike environment. The most important aspect that people express when involved in some way with residents living in a CADE environment is that the living conditions help to give the resident dignity, individual expression and freedom of movement regardless of the level of their dementia.

Total quality management questionnaires have involved relatives and staff. The outcomes have been favourable. Continuum of care is reviewed through meetings and resident reviews. The staff retention rate has remained constant. A large majority of employees have worked at the unit since it opened five years ago.

EDITORS' COMMENTS
The nine Confused and Disturbed Elderly units in NSW have an important place in the Australian thinking on designing for people with dementia. The CADE units were a response to the need to de-institutionalise older people with dementia, primarily those with challenging behaviours, and the CADE units reflect this focus upon behaviour management. These origins are important. The CADE units were the first physical structures to include a number of design features which assist in creating an environment in which previous and appropriate learned behaviour can be recalled, practised and rewarded. These are exemplified in Riverview Lodge.

First, the simple environment is small, with two mirror-image wings of eight units. Second, familiar domestic furnishings and decor were introduced, most notably in the communal areas.

Third – and perhaps most importantly – Riverview Lodge gives full expression to the concept "total visual access" with no corridors and all bedrooms opening onto the lounge and dining area. Every resident is able to know, sense or see where they are or where they want to go from any point within the unit and from the garden. At the same time the personal care staff can readily see residents.

Fourth, the philosophy that stimuli which are important to the resident are enhanced, while extraneous and potentially distracting stimuli have been reduced, is central to the CADE design.

Fifth, the provision of a simple garden area where residents can safely walk, tend the garden or sit, was also an important design development of the CADE units.

Flynn Lodge

Reasons for selection

- *Exceptional focus on client profile* • *Attempt to provide for radically different groups: indigenous and white Australians* • *Flexibility allows for differing levels of involvement in building: sociability and privacy* • *Bedrooms allow for single or double use* • *Strong relationship with external landscape* • *All bedrooms have direct access to secure gardens*

Flynn Lodge
Old Timers
Stuart Highway
Alice Springs NT 0870
Australia
Tel: (+61) 8 8952 2844
Fax: (+61) 8 8955 5225

Owner and managing organisation
Frontier Services, Uniting Church in Australia

Contact person for further information
Ms Sharon Davis
Executive Director of Nursing
Frontier Services
Old Timers
Stuart Highway
Alice Springs NT 0871

Type of building
Hostel for frail older people. Ten places are specifically provided for people who are confused and disturbed.

Architect
KLCK Architects
PO Box 1092
Collingwood VIC 3066
Tel: (+61) 3 9419 0299
Contact: Kirsty Bennett

Resident/client profile
Ambulant, with highly challenging behaviours and levels of confusion.

DESCRIPTION OF BUILDING

Site context
The site for Flynn Lodge is located through Heavitree Gap, a short distance from the town of Alice Springs. It is remote from the residential area of Alice Springs and instead is in a rural setting with a large area of land which fronts the Todd River.

Number of resident beds
20

Number of respite or assessment beds
None

Details of other overnight accommodation
Accommodation for family members, guests or staff is located elsewhere on the Old Timers site in detached cottages.

Plan form
The plan of Flynn Lodge consists of two clusters

Above, a view of Flynn Lodge from across the Todd River. Right, the approach and entry.

Design for Dementia

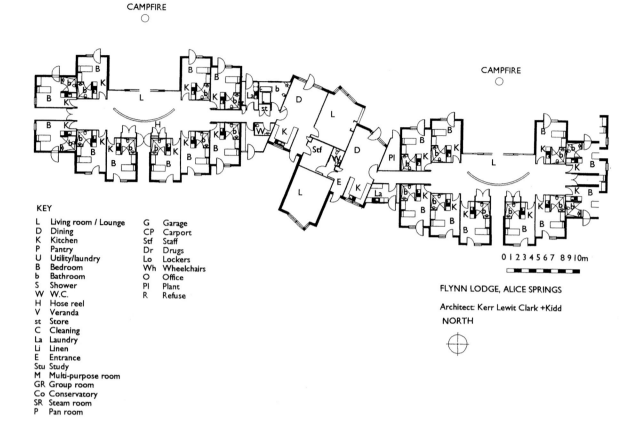

CAMPFIRE

CAMPFIRE

KEY

L	Living room / Lounge	G	Garage
D	Dining	CP	Carport
K	Kitchen	Stf	Staff
P	Pantry	Dr	Drugs
U	Utility/laundry	Lo	Lockers
B	Bedroom	Wh	Wheelchairs
b	Bathroom	O	Office
S	Shower	Pl	Plant
W	W.C.	R	Refuse
H	Hose reel		
V	Veranda		
st	Store		
C	Cleaning		
La	Laundry		
Li	Linen		
E	Entrance		
Stu	Study		
M	Multi-purpose room		
GR	Group room		
Co	Conservatory		
SR	Steam room		
P	Pan room		

0 1 2 3 4 5 6 7 8 9 10m

FLYNN LODGE, ALICE SPRINGS

Architect: Kerr Lewit Clark +Kidd

NORTH

of ten residents with completely separate facilities. "Mountview", the western cluster, has been designated for people with dementia and the two units are linked internally by a staff area.

Communal and shared spaces for residents

Each cluster has its own kitchen, dining room and lounge room. In addition, all bedrooms open onto a central indoor/outdoor sitting area.

The unit which will cater specifically for people with dementia has a bathroom and a separate WC adjacent to the dining room. A domestic-style laundry is also provided in this unit.

Staff facilities

A staff room is located in the centre of the hostel and provides the only internal link between the two clusters. This room provides a place for staff to relax.

Toilet facilities are also provided in this area. Additional staff facilities are located in the nursing home which is a short distance away.

Office and administration space

The staff room also functions as an office for the hostel supervisor. Administration services are otherwise performed in an adjacent administration centre.

Service and ancillary spaces

Service areas are located adjacent to the bedroom areas. Located conveniently for the use of staff and residents, these parts of the building also form an important visual separation between the different parts of the hostel.

What site constraints or external factors, such as existing buildings or local planning legislation, affected the form and planning of the building?

The building is designed to respond to the views which dominate the site, with every room looking out to either the Todd River or to the surrounding mountain ranges.

In addition, designing for passive thermal control has been of the utmost importance to minimise heat gain in the hostel, particularly in summer, autumn and spring.

Construction and external materials

The building has a steel roof structure set on columns. Built on a concrete slab, the walls are concrete block veneer with steel studs. The roof sheeting is corrugated iron.

Type(s) of flooring

Carpet is used in all bedroom areas (including kitchenettes), corridors, lounges, dining rooms and entries. Non-slip vinyl has been used in the kitchens, laundries, soiled utilities, bathroom and en suites. Vitrified tiles have been laid in the sitting rooms.

Internal finishes

Walls and ceilings have been lined with plasterboard throughout, with the exception of the sitting room which has exposed ply sheets with recessed joints. Walls in this area have a textured paint finish. Water-resistant plasterboard is used in wet areas such as en suites and bathrooms and these have a tiled finish.

Acoustic insulation has been provided between all bedrooms and between bedrooms and corridors.

Equipment

Flushing rim sinks for soiled utilities. A portable lifter will be used in the bathroom.

STAFFING

Management staff
0.5 FTE

Care staff
7.0 FTE

Other staff
26 hours per week

BUILDING STATISTICS

Site area within site boundaries
8,000m²

Ground floor area i.e. "footprint"
1,020m²

Total floor area
1,020m²

Floor area of individual units of accommodation
23.54m² per room

Floor area of common living and dining rooms per group or cluster as appropriate (excluding separate circulation space and corridors)
255.18m² Unit A & B (127.59 each)

Building cost including fixed equipment, hard and soft landscaping (but excluding loose furniture and fittings and professional fees)
A$1,721,733

BUILDING DESIGN

The philosophy of care

- To provide the kind of environment that encourages residents, guests and staff to treat it as the resident's home of choice.
- To promote independence by providing necessary support to build on strengths and minimise weaknesses of individual residents.
- To provide a safe environment for residents, staff and visitors.

How was the philosophy expressed in the design of the building?

- The concept of a group of individual dwellings that coexist rather than one large building;
- the integration of internal and external living areas;
- individual suites including bathrooms and kitchenettes;
- provision for couples and partners;
- choices in control of air temperatures;
- lack of "fixed staff call point" in suites and living areas;
- open plan kitchens;
- choices in living spaces e.g. lounge and sitting rooms;
- providing large landscaped grounds, including orchard and vegetable gardens, with direct external access from the residents' unit;
- individual kitchenettes for residents and guests;
- provision of space in kitchenettes for personal refrigerators;
- colour cueing, both internal and external;
- individual colour schemes for suites and furnishings;
- en suite bathrooms are all decorated as in private homes;
- unique main bathroom design incorporating timber;
- all external doors can be secured from the staff centre.

Approach to design

In addition to designing specifically for the needs of people with dementia, the approach to the design of Flynn Lodge has been influenced by a number of goals and beliefs such as: (a) the need for a flexible environment; (b) designing for people's abilities; (c) the provision of a homelike environment; and (d) allowing for privacy. These are elaborated upon below.

Key design principles

In addition, a number of broad principles have been identified which are important in the building design. These include:

- People in the Territory value their independence greatly.
- They also have diverse lifestyles and backgrounds and, as a result, the recognition of individuality is very important.

The building will need to be flexible. In addition to the elements mentioned above, the sheer size of the Territory, and the catchment area for residents, means that the hostel will need to be flexible to cater for differing levels of frailty and needs since alternative accommodation is often not available to residents. It is appropriate for the hostel to allow for different levels of involvement in the building. Some residents come from lifestyles where built structures are not significant, while others may have lived in a very urban environment. As a result, residents prefer to be involved in the building to a greater or lesser extent.

Given the different lifestyles of residents it is important that the hostel allows residents a variety of opportunities. The hostel should have a distinctive identity of its own, rather than being seen as an adjunct to the nursing home which is on the site. This is important in creating an image for the residents and the wider community which emphasises that the role and nature of this part of the site is quite different from the nursing home.

When housing 20 people together it is important to "break up" the facility to create a suitable scale, so that people are able to relate to a smaller and more intimate number of people. This is crucial in creating a residential and homelike environment: most people do not live with 20 others.

It is important that the staff have direct and easy access to each of the residential units while at the same time not eroding the individual resident's right to privacy within their "home". However, access by other people should be controlled so that strangers are not able to walk through the hostel and impinge upon residents' space.

Siting

Flynn Lodge is dominated by the hills which surround the area and can be seen in all directions. The site itself is relatively flat. There are a number of mature trees on the site and these include palms, pepper trees, cedars, jacarandas, mulgas and melaleucas. Cool breezes come from the south and east, but the summer north winds are very hot.

The building has been sited to maximise the views from the building and to provide a thermally efficient building. Flynn Lodge seeks to respond to the external environment through the orientation of the building and the provision of external nooks and sitting areas, which will allow residents to take advantage of the winter sun and the summer shade.

External character and appearance

The hostel is a community of buildings, rather than a building mass. The image of the cottages which have been on the Old Timers site for a long time is a positive one, and the hostel will use this imagery to reflect the different people and communities who will be living in the hostel.

The hostel does not dominate the landscape, but rather "disappears" or "dissipates" into it. Attention has been given to the edges of the building, so that the internal environment flows to the outside, and the external environment flows in. The hostel seeks to respond to the external environment through the orientation of the building and the provision of external nooks and sitting areas, which will allow residents to take advantage of the winter sun and the summer shade.

Above, special features at Flynn Lodge include paths which have been designed to lead walkers back to social spaces. Below, residents' communal spaces.

Design for Dementia

Above, a corridor links the sitting area with a kitchen and dining room. Note the cueing to assist in decision making. Below, special features include colour coding of bedrooms to provide clear choices.

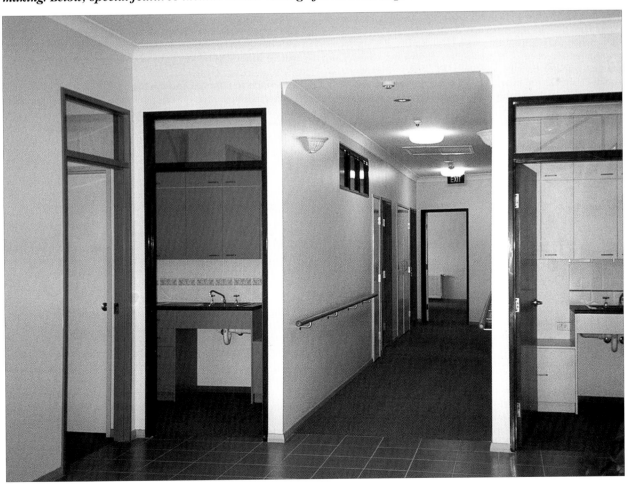

Plan form

The plan of Flynn Lodge is based around the concept of allowing people to move through the hostel and have different levels of involvement in the building. This is expressed in the way residents are able to choose to spend more time outside than inside, to be in a more formal part of the building (such as the lounge room) or in a less structured area (such as the sitting area), to be with others, or to be by themselves.

The hostel at Old Timers' is designed as two clusters of ten independent living units, rather than as one or two "houses". While people of diverse backgrounds are expected to live side by side, it is recognised that they may not wish to share their lives on a day-to-day basis.

Entry

The primary entry leads to a domestic kitchen and dining room. The entry is a discrete area where people can be greeted without interrupting the life of the residents.

In addition, secondary entries are provided to each of the bedroom units. The "front doors" of the units open onto the gardens while the back door opens onto the sitting area.

Transition space

Very little space has been provided solely for the purpose of transition. Transition spaces fulfil an important role as they act as a buffer between residents' private areas and social areas, allowing privacy for residents and an efficient link between different parts of the building and the external environment.

Choices in movement through the building are provided by the creation of different travel paths, some internal and others external. This allows people to move through the building in different ways, to associate with different people and to approach the building from a number of points.

En suites

Separate en suites have been provided for each resident. This recognises the need for privacy for all people and the different life experiences of the residents. Belongings which are very precious to one person will not be for another, for example talcum powder and soap may be of great value to one resident while for others a digging stick and a blanket are more important. The size of the en suites allows for wheelchair manoeuvrability. En suites contain a WC, step-free shower and basin. Grab rails are provided and separate hot and cold taps have been installed (rather than a mixer which is likely to be unfamiliar and confusing). Taps are located to the side of the shower rather than under the rose. Flooring is non-slip vinyl.

Bedrooms

Bedrooms take the form of independent units. This allows people the opportunity to decide if they want to join in the life of the hostel, and will give them the flexibility to continue their lifestyle with the people they choose to. An important feature is that a number of rooms are linked by interlocking doors for use by couples, siblings or friends.

All the rooms have large windows with a view to the surrounding countryside. There is direct access from each room to the outdoors, with step-free porches so that people can sit outside their rooms. (Doors are able to be locked to stop people coming in as well as people going out).

Bedrooms are large enough to accommodate chairs and other furniture, or to allow for more than one mattress or bed as many Aboriginal people like to share a room with others. Beds can be lowered right down to accommodate people who need to sleep near the floor while providing a suitable working environment for staff.

The inclusion of kitchenettes to bedrooms further enhances people's independence and privacy. A microwave, small fridge and sink are provided in each bedroom. The height of the fridge and microwave is appropriate for ease of use. Surfaces in the bedrooms are washable. Built-in cupboard space is provided to give people a place for their clothes and possessions.

Kitchen/dining

Separate domestic kitchens for each cluster of ten hostel residents are provided. Cooking facilities are at a height which is suitable for older people so that they are not required to bend to reach the oven or microwave.

Social spaces

Social spaces are situated at the ends of each cluster. The bay window in the lounge enables people to look out at the river and the mountains, and an open fire is provided as people like to be able to sit and watch a fire. A large sitting area which is open to outside by day and is not heated or cooled by artificial means is located at the opposite end of the cluster.

While the lounge is more formal, the sitting area at the other end of the cluster is a two-storey space with a curved ply ceiling. Residents are therefore given a choice about the environment they wish to use: small or large, formal or informal, private or communal, artificially or naturally heated and cooled.

Bathroom

Attention has been given to creating a bathroom which is welcoming and friendly, as many people with dementia feel threatened when faced with a large and imposing bathroom. Timber has been introduced to create a feeling of warmth in the room. A slatted timber bench has been built to one side of the spa bath so that access can be provided for staff when assistance is required, while reinforcing the small scale of the room at other times by masking this space.

Service areas

Service areas are placed adjacent to the social areas. Located conveniently for the use of staff and residents off transition spaces, these parts of the building also form an important visual separation between the different parts of the hostel.

Approach and entrance

All access to the hostel for people with dementia is via the front door of people's bedrooms which each have an external address. It is important to emphasise that the front door will also be the main entry point for the cluster housing residents with dementia, as access to and from this part of the hostel will be controlled by key pads and discreet fencing.

Approach to signage and cueing

Signage has been minimised at Flynn Lodge. Cueing has been provided through the use of colour, the use of familiar items, the provision of personal items, and the use of view.

Enabling residents to make a clear choice is a vital element of cueing. This is seen in the placing of the bedrooms around a central sitting area so that residents are faced with a clear choice upon leaving their rooms: either proceed along the short corridor and enter the dining/kitchen areas or go outside (where the paths also lead back to these social spaces).

Approach to colour schemes and interior design

Each cluster within Flynn Lodge has a dominant colour which is seen in the social spaces and corridors. Residents' rooms are then selected from a range of colours, with no two rooms having the same tiles, carpet, or paint colour (although these have in fact been chosen from a limited range).

The emphasis on the interior design of Flynn Lodge is to use a range of colours in different combinations, therefore creating very different effects while restricting the number of colours which are used in the building.

Bedrooms have been furnished to provide residents with choice. Different styles and levels of detail have been provided in the furnishings, with some rooms featuring strong solid woven fabrics while others are decorated with florals.

As one moves through the building the finishes become more traditional, with the sitting areas featuring simple woven curtains and the lounges containing decorative curtains which have been carefully coordinated with the furniture.

Security provisions

The relationship between the site, its surroundings, and the changing directional views is one of the most important features of the hostel site. For this reason much attention has been given to the treatment of the site perimeter. It is proposed to retain the sense of openness which characterises the existing landscape, while at the same time bringing the distant landscape closer by echoing some of its characteristics in the hostel environs.

Fencing is designed to be transparent. *Eucalyptus camaldulensis* (river red gum) will be planted to the north-east of the hostel building so that the landscape of the Todd River continues on the site and the boundary between the hostel landscape and wider landscape is blurred. Along the western boundary of the site the highway surface will be screened by low shrubs and ground cover, while maintaining the view to the distant ranges.

Security is provided within the building through a system of electronic locks to external bedroom doors which allows staff to close and lock all doors at a certain time. Each door can be overridden by the use of a key to allow residents unrestrained access as desired. Reed switches allow the constant monitoring of the doors from the staff area and the link between the locks, reed switches and staff call system ensures that this is simple and efficient while respecting residents' independence and privacy. Internally access from other buildings is controlled by a key pad.

Heating and/or ventilation system or air conditioning system

Each bedroom is provided with evaporative cooling. A ceiling fan and openable windows provide cross ventilation to allow residents maximum choice and control of their environments. Hydronic heating is also installed.

Social spaces generally are provided with evaporative cooling and hydronic heating, with the exception of the indoor/outdoor sitting space which responds to the natural environment and relies on passive solar design and cross ventilation for heating and cooling.

Key principles of design

A number of key principles have been adopted in the design of the hostel. These include the provision of a flexible environment, designing for abilities, the provision of a homelike environment, allowing for privacy, and designing for dementia.

Flexibility

Flexibility is essential in the design of the hostel. Residents will come from a diverse range of experiences and backgrounds, and a flexible environment will be required to ensure that their various needs are met.

Many Aboriginal people in Central Australia have traditional lifestyles and don't identify with buildings as non-Aboriginal people do. Areas will be used quite differently and it will be important that spaces can be appropriated by the user during their stay in the hostel.

Accessibility

It is important to allow for residents' residual abilities to be maximised through an enabling environment. It is expected that many of the residents will have a higher level of physical disability than is usually seen, as members of the Aboriginal community are likely to have a significant vision impairment and severe mobility problems.

Deficits caused by elderly people's diminished physical, sensory, or mental abilities need to be recognised, and essential supports incorporated in a subtle manner. All areas need to be wheelchair accessible and attention needs to be given to the height of elements so that they are accessible for all users.

Special attention has been given to lighting levels and acoustic treatments to enhance communication. While the environment must eliminate hazards, it must also induce a feeling of competence in the resident: it must allow for challenges and risk-taking.

Homelike environment

A homelike environment emphasises a feeling of warmth and security, familiarity and independence. It is usually relatively small in scale with familiar details, minimum distances and familiar relationships. It also involves decision-making and choice, and control over one's own life.

A homelike environment cannot be categorised or prescribed, as it is not the same for all people and is governed by a person's previous experiences and expectations.

It is important to understand that people use spaces and buildings differently. An Aboriginal person, for example, will sit in the shade of the house to get out of the sun rather than going inside. The house will be seen as an object casting a shadow, rather than as an environment which can provide protection. In winter, an Aboriginal person will use the house to seek shelter from freezing breezes, by sitting outside and using the house as a windbreak while they receive warmth from an open fire and from the sun.

A house is often valued as a place of security and as a place where things can be left.

Privacy and community living

A balance between private and communal space will be essential. Independence is very strong in the Territory. There are not many houses in town with three or four old people living together, and non-Aboriginal people generally do not live communally. Most of the people that the hostel will cater for are of old stock: they are very independent and privacy is important.

Privacy is not such an issue for Aboriginal people "out bush" where everything is settled in public. This is a way of life that is not common for non-Aboriginal people and can be quite stifling for them. Aboriginal people will often draw a semi-circle with a fire at its centre and spaces radiating out from this to illustrate their preferred living arrangement. This allows people to sit at the fire and share in the community, and then withdraw, yet still be in touch. Public living will be important to the older Aboriginal people so that they don't lose contact with each other and with what is going on. It is important for Aboriginal people to be able to see everyone else. It is likely that these residents will prefer to use the part of the building which gives the greatest view.

Aboriginal people don't like to be by themselves. It is important for Aboriginal people to be able to share bedrooms if they choose to. Privacy between tribes and between men and women will, however, need to be accommodated.

While residents of different backgrounds can live side by side, it is not appropriate that they are asked to share facilities as neither person will feel comfortable.

Dementia

When designing for people with dementia it is essential to provide an environment which enables residents to use their remaining cognitive abilities and skills to the highest possible level. To achieve this, the principles of redundant cueing, wayfinding and orientation, familiarity, scale and security need to be pursued.

People with dementia need open space, and the external environment needs to provide opportunities which are familiar and satisfying. Trees, fires, sitting areas and gardens are part of this. People need to be able to move about, and fencing needs to be provided in a non-restrictive manner.

KEY FEATURES OF FLYNN LODGE

Entry

The "front doors" of the units open onto the gardens. The back door opens onto a transition space. Staff will be able to use this route, but this space will also fulfil an important role as it acts as a buffer between residents' private areas and social areas.

The provision of a designated entry for each of the hostel clusters is essential. It is important not to enter through a lounge or dining room.

Transition space

Choices in movement through the building will be provided by the creation of different travel paths, some which are internal and others which are external. This will allow people to move through the building in different ways, to associate with different people and to approach the building from a number of points. Transition spaces will allow privacy for residents and an efficient link between different parts of the building.

En suites

Separate en suites have been provided for each resident. It is important to recognise the need for privacy for all people and the different life experiences of the residents. Belongings which are very precious to one person will not be for another, for example talcum powder and soap may be of great value to one resident while for others a digging stick and a blanket are more important.

The size of the en suites allows for wheelchair manoeuvrability. En suites contain WC, shower and basin. Grab rails are provided and taps are lever taps.

Separate hot and cold taps have been installed (rather than a mixer), and these are located to the side of the shower rather than under the rose. The shower is step free. Heating is provided in the en suites. Non-slip flooring is essential.

Bedrooms

Bedrooms take the form of independent units. This will allow people the opportunity to decide if they want to join in the life of the hostel, and will give them the flexibility to continue their lifestyle with the people they choose to.

The rooms have large windows looking to a view outside. There is direct outside access from each room, with step-free

Above, the kitchen/dining area. Below, a resident's personal space – a typical bedroom.

Above, the lounge at Flynn Lodge. Below, a welcoming bathroom.

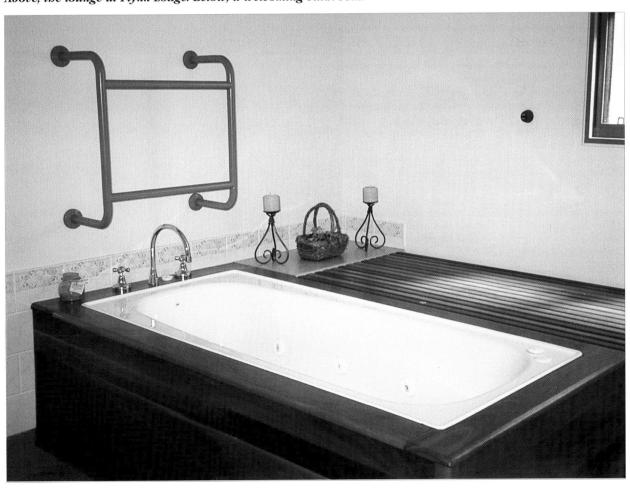

porches so that people can sit outside their rooms, either in a garden setting or on the sand. Security at night is important and doors can be closed to stop people coming in (as well as people going out).

As a number of people spend a lot of time in their bedrooms it is important to be able to accommodate chairs and other furniture. It is important to recognise that Aboriginal people like to share with others from their own tribe, and so the possibility of more than one mattress or bed in each bedroom is important.

The inclusion of kitchenettes to bedrooms further enhances people's independence and privacy. A microwave, small fridge and sink are provided in each bedroom. The fridge and microwave are at a convenient height for ease of use. Surfaces in the bedrooms are washable. Cupboard space is provided for clothes and possessions.

A number of residents are likely to prefer sleeping on a mattress on the floor rather than in a bed. Beds are able to go down to a low height to accommodate this need.

Some rooms with interconnecting doors are for use by couples, sisters or friends.

Kitchen/Dining
Separate domestic kitchens for each cluster of ten hostel residents are provided. Cooking facilities are at a height which is suitable for older people so that they are not required to bend to reach the oven or microwave.

Lounge
The lounges provide residents with a more formal sitting area. Views from the lounge enable people to look to the river and the mountains. An open fire inside is important as people like to be able to sit and watch the fire.

A variety of lounge chairs are provided to suit different tastes. People need to be able to get out of them easily, and so the arms are firm.

Success in meeting intentions
Unfortunately at time of completing this report the building is not occupied.

Major hurdles that had to be overcome or prevented the intentions from being achieved
It is anticipated that the occupancy will begin in April and staff recruitment has commenced. The major hurdle anticipated is staff preconceptions of what is "support" and what is "care". The building will work well with adequate education of staff and relatives/friends of residents who will require assistance to work through the concept of supporting people with dementia and allowing risk-taking and providing choice wherever practicable, rather than the traditional custodial care model.

Aspects of the building design worthy of replication?
All aspects where designed to meet the needs of the diverse cultural backgrounds of the Central Australian client group.
To be avoided in the future ?
None.

EDITORS' COMMENTS
If any facility in this book challenges us to look first at who is our client, it is Old Timers' hostel in Alice Springs, Northern Territory. This design has sought to recognise that people in the Northern Territory have diverse lifestyles and backgrounds. There are Aboriginals and whites, town and country folk. They value their independence greatly and regardless of race have a strong relationship with the environment. Some come from lifestyles where built structures are not significant, while others may be more urbanised. Some are tribal and communal; others are loners. And there are not many of them in a Territory the size of continental Europe. The design has taken into account that the hostel will need to cater for differ-

ing levels of frailty and need because alternative accommodation will simply not be available.

This has produced a flexible building which allows for residents to have different levels of involvement in the building. Some will prefer to spend their time outside under the shade of a tree; others will be comfortable in a more formal lounge room. The facility is "broken up" to a suitable scale so that two groups of ten people can relate communally or simply be private, concepts which are applicable to different cultural groups.

The entire building is oriented to the landscape which, for indigenous people, is culturally such a significant part of them and, for white people, has held a lifelong attraction. Many of the residents are more comfortable sitting on the ground outside and the house is where you keep valuable things: there is even provision for them to sit inside as if they were outside.

Annalakoti + Pekkalakoti

Reasons for selection

- Development of floor plan already used at Impivaarakoti
- Linking of two units which share facilities • Commitment to shared rooms
- Sensitive handling of campus approach

Annalakoti + Pekkalakoti
Sukkavartaankatu 9 3310
Tampere
Finland
Tel: (+ 358) 3 2141 377
Fax: (+ 358) 3 2146 887

Owner and managing organisation
Sopimusvuori Foundation

Contact person for further information
Päivi Karjalainen

Type of building
Nursing home/group home for people with dementia

Architect
Lairto

Resident/client profile
Ambulant, and non-ambulant with highly challenging behaviours.
Ambulant, with levels of confusion

DESCRIPTION OF BUILDING

Site context
The homes are situated within the confines of the City of Tampere in small residential estates comprising of detached houses about six kilometres from the central of the city.

Number of resident beds
11 (Annalakoti) + 10 (Pekkalakoti)

Number of respite or assessment beds
One bed for short time (2-3 months) use.

Details of other overnight accommodation
No overnight accommodation for staff, one guest room for friends and relatives for overnight stays.

Plan form
Two group homes (11 beds + 10 beds), connected with each other.

Communal and shared spaces for residents
See floor plan.

Staff facilities
Dressing room and toilet.

Office and administration space
No separate office. Administration space for staff only.

Service and ancillary spaces
See floor plan.

What site constraints or external factors, such as existing buildings or local planning legislation, affected the form and planning of the building?
Permitted building volume and the type of buildings already in that area.

Construction and external materials
Wooden, partly brick-faced, semi-detached house with a tin roof.

Type(s) of flooring
All other rooms are covered with linoleum but in the sauna and bathrooms/toilets there is non-slip vinyl floor covering or clinker. Beside every resident's beds is the same electric alarm system as we have in our new nursing homes. Floor heating in toilets.

Internal finishes
Cyproc with wallpapers, wooden ceilings, tiled walls in bathrooms/toilets.

Equipment
Special equipment in sauna and in bathrooms/toilets (handrails, shower chairs, lowered sauna benches). Rooms (living rooms) are fully-furnished with beautiful heavy old furniture so that residents can take support and it encourages residents to walk. No central kitchen – all food is made in the common kitchen and residents are encouraged to participate in any daily household chores depending on their abilities and needs. Ordinary kitchen tools are used.

STAFFING

Management staff
One director in both group houses
Care staff
Five in each house plus other staff members
Other staff
A few volunteers, friends and relatives, but not on a regular basis.

Design for Dementia

73

Above, the drive and entrance to Annalakoti and Pekkalakoti. Below, residents enjoying the garden in summer.

Above, a communal gathering on the garden terrace. Below, working in the kitchen.

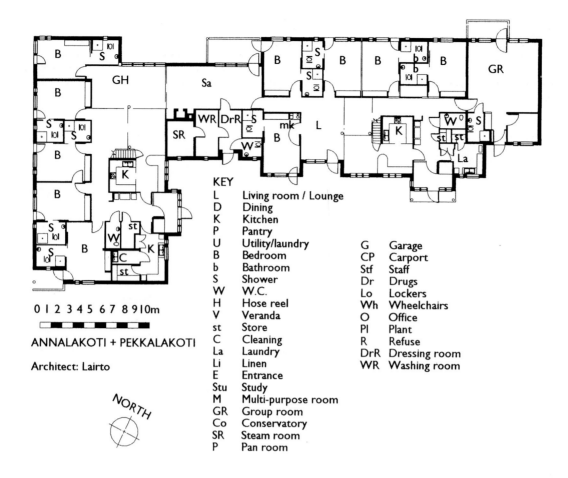

KEY

L	Living room / Lounge
D	Dining
K	Kitchen
P	Pantry
U	Utility/laundry
B	Bedroom
b	Bathroom
S	Shower
W	W.C.
H	Hose reel
V	Veranda
st	Store
C	Cleaning
La	Laundry
Li	Linen
E	Entrance
Stu	Study
M	Multi-purpose room
GR	Group room
Co	Conservatory
SR	Steam room
P	Pan room

G	Garage
CP	Carport
Stf	Staff
Dr	Drugs
Lo	Lockers
Wh	Wheelchairs
O	Office
Pl	Plant
R	Refuse
DrR	Dressing room
WR	Washing room

0 1 2 3 4 5 6 7 8 9 10m

ANNALAKOTI + PEKKALAKOTI

Architect: Lairto

NORTH

BUILDING STATISTICS

Site area within site boundaries
Site area 9400m² (one rehabilitation home and four nursing homes). Small residential estates comprising detached houses .

Ground floor area i.e. "footprint"
242m² (Annalakoti) + 227m² (Pekkalakoti) + 63m² common sauna department plus a group room/visitors room with kitchen facilities 56m².

Total floor area
As above

Building cost including fixed equipment, hard and soft landscaping (but excluding loose furniture and fittings and professional fees)
4.5 million Finnish marks (FIM) for both homes.

BUILDING DESIGN

The philosophy of care
The basic idea of the Sopimusvuori Foundation is to develop all its homes into a therapeutic community.

For example residents are encouraged to participate in any daily household chores depending on their abilities and needs, meals are shared and there are no coffee/lunch hours for staff members, no locked offices or other doors except the front door in the winter or the gate door in the summer.

It is important that the homes provide the necessary care for the rest of the resident's life unless special medical care is required.

Anxiety, frustration, aggression and depression – the usual symptoms of dementia – are treated with high doses of sedatives in large nursing homes. In our small group homes it is possible to focus our attention on every resident as an individual. The therapeutic community gives a safe and secure environment so the usual symptoms rarely occur and the need for sedatives is rather small.

How was the philosophy expressed in the design of the building?

Internally

For residents: as few corridors as possible. Most of the bedrooms open onto the sitting room, meals are prepared and eaten together, there is home-like old furniture, no locked doors. Rooms (living rooms) are quite fully furnished with heavy old furniture so that residents can use it for support which encourages them to walk.

Relatives and friends are always welcome to visit and participate in any activities. It is also possible for them to stay overnight in another nursing home nearby.

Externally

For residents: a group home looks like other small houses in the same area and homelike living is the main idea. Residents can walk around the garden, the front door is not locked in the summer although the gate door is.

Relatives and friends are always welcome. There are no set visiting hours and all the group's homes have good public transport connections.

For staff: The Sopimusvuori Foundation has its own course centre and all staff members are trained to our philosophy. It is important that group homes have contacts with the neighbourhood, nearby schools, etc.

Plan form
Two similar units linked to share sauna. All rooms are doubles with en suite facilities. All rooms enjoy good visual access with communal spaces.

Siting

The home is situated within the confines of the city of Tampere about six kilometres from the city centre, in a small residential estate of detached houses.

External character and appearance

A home that looks like any of the other small houses in the area.

Approach and entrance

See picture.

Approach to signage and cueing

Most of the bedrooms open on to the sitting room. There is a round corridor. Residents' first names are in big block letters on the doors of their bedrooms. The sitting room and dining room are open space and easy to find.

Approach to colour schemes and interior design

Rooms, such as the living room, are fully furnished with beautiful heavy old furniture that residents can use for support which encourages them to walk. Special attention has been paid to ensure that the building is light and clear and as "homelike" as possible. Windows are at a height that residents can see out of when sitting.

Security provisions

A special electrical alarm system is installed under the floor in front of beds. This system has been installed in all the group's home. (See Impivaarakoti.)

The gate to the house is kept locked.

Heating and/or ventilation system or air conditioning system

District heating. There is an air-conditioning system which stores up the heat.

Technology used

Electrical wooden beds and a special electrical alarm system under the floor in front of beds.

Success in meeting intentions

In all aspects.

Major hurdles that had to be overcome or prevented the intentions from being achieved

Money.

Aspects of the building design worthy of replication?

At present we are building two new group homes and we are using the information we have gained from the eight homes we already have (the first was founded in 1991) and also the information from the STAKES research mentioned above.

To be avoided in the future?

No more single rooms. Old people have lived most of their lives with other people and shared their bedrooms with their husbands or wives and they feel more safe when they can hear somebody's breathing nearby.

Feedback

STAKES and the Sopimusvuori Foundation have studied the ground plan's effect on the quality but also on the cost of the care. This research studied 12 different units, both from traditional big nursing homes and from small group homes. The aim was to encourage politicians and staff members to pay attention to how much the environment affects, and also improves, the quality of the care. The staff of the 12 units were interviewed and 38 residents were observed in this research. This information was used when drawing up the plan form of the two new homes.

EDITORS' COMMENTS

Annalakoti and Pekkalakoti are linked houses adjoining two similar houses served by a private drive in a residential suburb. It was built after Impivaarakoti and is the result of the experience gained there. Both houses have five double rooms arranged around a central space which contains the kitchen, which like Impivaarakoti, is part of the circulation space. All rooms are doubles and have en suite shower rooms

Each house has its own entrance, its own kitchen and laundry. The only shared facility which forms a link between the two houses, is the sauna department which, with ancillary accommodation, sitting area, WC and circulation, occupies approx. 63m^2.

The Sopimusvuori Foundation is of the view that the majority of people like to share. Most people have shared a bedroom for a large part of their lives. Whether or not this has been established by objective research is not clear. Hence, however, the decision to have only double bedrooms which goes with the change to en suite shower rooms throughout.

The comparison with Impivaarakoti, which provides a touchstone as far as providing a genuinely homely, non institutional environment is concerned, is very interesting.

A small campus, with a gated entrance, consisting of four buildings including Annalakoti + Pekkalakoti, accommodates a group of 60 residents and 31 staff. Because of the small size of the campus all the buildings can have a proportion of their rooms looking outwards overlooking the surrounding roads and houses.

The floor plan is similar in principle to Impivaarakoti, a rectangular communal space in the centre with the bedrooms arranged along one side and the entrance and other facilities, including a generous shared sauna facility, around the other two sides. The kitchen is placed within the space but to one end with circulation both around and through it. This creates a living room which can be seen from the door of each bedroom. The slope of the roof over the living room is utilised to create an additional gallery area over the kitchen reached by a staircase. Daylighting to the living room is supplemented by the roof lights to this space.

The two houses are similar but not identical. Annalakoti has a living room overlooking the gardens of adjoining houses, Pekkalakoti's living room overlooks the entrance drive. The space standards, measured in terms of total floor area per person show an increase over Impivaarakoti from 23m^2 per person to 27m^2 excluding the gallery.

The differences, by comparison with Impivaarakoti, have a major impact on the way the houses are perceived both by their location and their internal character. The creation of a gated campus, the introduction of the sloping ceiling, the daylighting through the roof and the first floor gallery within the volume of the living room all tend to destroy the normality of Impivaarakoti in its relationship to the outside world and its attractive domesticity internally.

The question to be asked what has driven these changes, cost considerations, a desire for greater efficiency and economies of scale or a simple and laudable desire to improve things? It would be interesting to know because it strikes at the heart of what designing for dementia is about and defining the way forward.

Sidegate Lane

Reasons for selection

- *Excellent-sized bedrooms allowing own furniture* • *Well-designed bathrooms*
- *Generous communal spaces, such as the conservatory* • *Accessible and interactive garden areas* • *'No names/address only' approach to relating to the neighbourhood*

Name and address of building
248 Sidegate Lane
Ipswich
Suffolk
IP4 3DH

Owner
Orbit Housing Association
14 St Mathews Rd
Norwich
Norfolk NR1 1SP
Tel: 01603 767286

Contact person for further information
Derek Player, Regional Director (Eastern)

Type of building
Nursing home

Architect
Roderick I. Rees
Rees Associates
Chapel House
Out Westgate
Bury St Edmunds
Suffolk IP33 3NZ
Tel: 01284-756166
Fax: 01284-702615

Resident/client profile
Ambulant and non-ambulant, both with highly challenging behaviours.

DESCRIPTION OF BUILDING

Site context
Suburban

The entrance to 248 Sidegate Lane – identifiable from the road, but not obtrusive.

Above, external view of the conservatory. Below, shared living room adjoining entrance.

Number of resident beds
23

Number of respite or assessment beds
1

Details of other overnight accommodation
Guest room.

Plan form
Three groups, each of eight residents.

Communal and shared spaces for residents
Three residents' sitting/dining areas, one main lounge, three assisted bathrooms, four wheelchair-use toilets, one hobbies room and one glazed conservatory.

Staff facilities
One staffroom, one shower, one WC, one drug store, one locker room and an interview room.

Office and administration space
One office.

Service and ancillary spaces
One kitchen with adjacent washing up area, one laundry, three sluice rooms, one lift, four linen store cupboards and five general store cupboards.

What site constraints or external factors (i.e. existing buildings, local planning legislation, etc.) affected the form and planning of the building?
Cruciform shaped site. Maximum dimensional requirements of building from site boundaries and minimal visual impact of building from road.

Construction and external materials
Insulated stock brick/block cavity walling, precast concrete insulated flooring, softwood, double-glazed casement windows, timber pitched roof trusses with concrete interlocking pantiles.

Type(s) of flooring
Vinyl sheet safety flooring to all kitchen/bathroom areas with carpeting elsewhere.

Internal finishes
Two-coat plasterwork to walls, plasterboard with artex finish to ceilings.

Equipment
Two mobile manual operated lifting hoists; one electrically operated lifting hoist with built-in scales; three assisted bathrooms with two Parker Freedom baths and one Parker Madison (all with electrically operated hoist); two Pegasus pressure relieving mattresses; one Talley pressure relieving mattress; 12 Alpha pressure relieving mattresses, six Alpha pressure relieving cushions; two sluice rooms with macerators in each; 12 Hoskins beds (Kings Fund type); 12 electric head/foot elevating beds; one brush electrical carpet cleaner; one suction electrical carpet cleaner; 12 pressure pads linked to nurse call system. Two industrial washing machines; two industrial tumble dryers; one rotary iron; nurse call system with individual pagers plus various other standard nursing aids; large screen TVs, hi-fis etc.

STAFFING

Management staff

Manager	36.25hrs/wk
Deputy	37.50hrs/wk

Care staff

Trained staff:	6 x 37.5hrs/wk

Untrained staff:	1 x 22.5hrs/wk
	2 x 20hrs/wk
	1 x 30 hrs/wk
	13 x 30hrs/wk
	2 x 22.5 hrs/wk
	4 x 20hrs/wk

Other staff

Kitchen staff	101hrs/wk;
Domestic	68hrs/wk
Laundry	41hrs/wk
Gardener/handyman	30hrs/wk
Sec/admin assist	20 hrs/wk
Activities organiser	16 hr/wk

BUILDING STATISTICS

Site area within site boundaries
3,500m²

Ground floor area i.e. "footprint"
920m²

Total floor area
1192m²

Floor area of individual units of accommodation
16m²

Floor area of common living and dining rooms per group or cluster as appropriate (excluding separate circulation space and corridors)
41m²

Building cost including fixed equipment, hard and soft landscaping (but excluding loose furniture and fittings and professional fees)
£1,280,249

BUILDING DESIGN

The philosophy of care
To provide a high quality of care, dignity and understanding to older people suffering extreme mental health problems in an environment which is quiet, non-confrontational and peaceful, yet stimulating to a level which is relevant to resident needs. We also offer support and guidance for relatives and to include them in all aspects of the care of their relative.

How was the philosophy expressed in the design of the building?
Internally: There are several areas where residents can find space for themselves, such as corridors broken up by the use of seating areas. This creates corridors that do not look like corridors and provides meaningful areas for the wandering resident to walk to. Many "added features" within the building, such as the use of wood, shaped windows, etc., act as focal points of interest and comment for all.

Residents have individual bedrooms with a choice, in some, of interconnecting doors. All have en suite facilities. The emphasis is on creating as "homelike" an atmosphere as possible in every detail such as individual decoration in each bedroom.

There is a maximum of eight residents per unit/wing with their own bathroom, lounge, etc. This arrangement allows self-contained units of only eight but with an economical total figure of 24 beds. There is a large lounge for larger group functions with amenities to serve these functions and an integral kitchen for residents' meals only.

Lighting has been kept adjustable to meet the many and varied needs of both residents and staff.

SIDEGATE LANE
Ground floor

Architect: Rees Associates

0 1 2 3 4 5 6 7 8 9 10m

NORTH

KEY

L	Living room / Lounge
D	Dining
K	Kitchen
P	Pantry
U	Utility/laundry
B	Bedroom
b	Bathroom
S	Shower
W	W.C.
H	Hose reel
V	Veranda
st	Store
C	Cleaning
La	Laundry
Li	Linen
E	Entrance
Stu	Study
M	Multi-purpose room
GR	Group room

Co	Conservatory
SR	Steam room
P	Pan room
G	Garage
CP	Carport
Stf	Staff
Dr	Drugs
Lo	Lockers
Wh	Wheelchairs
O	Office
Pl	Plant
R	Refuse
F	Fire

The quiet areas are also appreciated by visiting friends and relatives since they provide privacy. Tea-making facilities are available at all times. Relatives are also reassured by aspects of the building design such as the key system, outside doors integrated with the nurse call system, etc. which provide a sense of safety. Staff appreciate the bright, spacious working environment and the provision of a separate staff area. They have enough room to separate noisy or disturbed residents for "time out" periods if required. There is also a large "walk in" clinic with ample cupboard space.

Externally, residents have been provided with a fully-enclosed safe garden area with age related/sensory stimulating features and a conservatory which looks out onto the car park and road, allowing residents to see "the outside world".

There is no name to the building, just an address which blends in with the locale thus avoiding any stigma for friends, relatives and members of the local community. From the road the building simply looks like a large bungalow.

Security lighting, a large and enclosed car park and a bike shed are among the external features provided for staff.

Siting
A new building set in a suburban, somewhat dull environment of 1930's housing.

Plan form
Each wing is expressed in the plan shape.

External character and appearance
New building to have its own identifiable character – but should not be obtrusive. Mixture of varying roof lines provides interest.

Approach and entrance
The entrance is clearly identifiable from the road, but the bulk of the main building is obscured from view.

Approach to signage and cueing
Written signage is kept to a minimum, including statutory ones. Visual cueing using colours and patterns is used instead.

Approach to colour schemes and interior design
Maximum emphasis has been placed on traditional domestic design to assist orientation. Coloured door furniture aids the location of sanitary facilities. There was a choice of six colours within the personal areas.

Security provisions
Emphasis has been placed on maximum freedom to wander safely within the building and garden within

SIDEGATE LANE
First floor

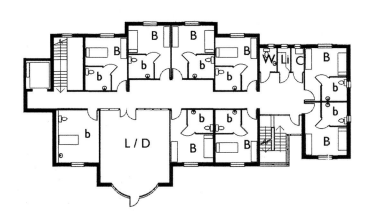

Design for Dementia

81

the perimeter fencing. Doors to hazardous areas are operated by high level levers. The coded front door releases with a speech mechanism.

Heating and/or ventilation system or air conditioning system

Floor and ceiling electric heating leaves walls free of obstructions. High level of natural and assisted ventilation ensures ample fresh air changes.

Technology used

There is a comprehensive wire-less nurse call system including staff pager operation and accessories such as pressure pads, door sensors, etc. Special baths cater for graded levels of dependency. A personal assessment system monitors resident well-being and abilities and ensures appropriate care levels to each individual.

Success in meeting intentions

Building achieves planning objective of retaining its own character within a somewhat ordinary suburban setting. Our core objectives were fully realised.

Major hurdles to be overcome

Irregular shaped site, virtually surrounded on all boundaries by other properties.

Aspects of the building design worthy of replication?

The emphasis on personal domestic space, overall internal environment and plan shape and the avoidance of institutional character.

To be avoided in the future?

Ideally the building would have been on one floor to avoid lift, stairs, etc. Kitchen and laundry have limited space.

Feedback

We get positive feedback from the people with dementia every day in our work. Friends and relatives are also very positive – although they have very little else to compare us with. We had a great deal of feedback from staff when first open. Little since. Generally it has been very positive.

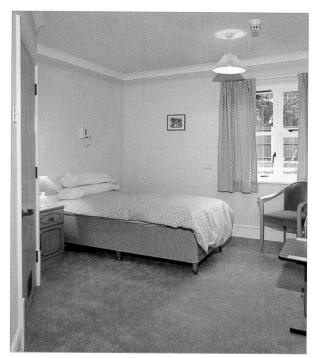

A typical resident's room with a wardrobe and an en suite shower on left.

EDITORS' COMMENTS

248 Sidegate Lane (the number rather than a name is intended to reduce the institutional overtones) appears a low one and two-storey building set well back from the road frontage in a quiet residential suburb. A parking area occupies the space in front of the building. This arrangement does separate the building from road and from the surrounding houses and in spite of the absence of a name it does signal "institution".

The entrance is into a foyer area and then via a generous common lounge off which is a small and very pleasant conservatory overlooking the entrance and car park. The foyer and lounge are pleasant, hotel like spaces and are in addition to the living dining rooms in the clusters.

Two of the three clusters are at ground level. Each cluster with eight residents with its own combined living and dining room, a small seating area and an assisted bathroom together with a separate WC is planned on both sides of a central corridor which widens in the centre opposite the glazed screen which separates the living room from the corridor. At the far end of the corridor from the entrance door small seating areas have been created. The ones in the centre are barely large enough to accommodate more than one person and on the upper floors the top lighting at high level under the ridge of the roof makes the space feel somewhat exposed. Whether these spaces are an amenity appreciated by residents or staff or introduce a non domestic or institutional character is a matter for debate.

Assisted bathrooms are generous in area and on outside walls with windows making them light attractive spaces. However, carers have noticed that, in spite of these positive design features, perhaps because of their size and hard finishes, residents are often disorientated, something that could be the result of the change of acoustics. Consideration is now being given to introducing absorbants, which could take the form of a cork covered wall or wall hangings.

The garden areas at Sidegate Lane are a delight, they are well planted and generous in area with a series of looping paths which take "wanderers" back into the building. However, there is an absence of direct connections between the living/dining rooms and the outside via French or patio doors which seriously limits the ability of residents to enjoy the open air and the sight, sounds and smells of nature.

A corridor of generous width is used to create a small sitting area. The living room is through the glazed screen on right.

Moorside

- *Excellent design on difficult, urban site* • *Strong relationship with community*
- *Good visual access with curved corridors* • *Generous garden given site constraints*
- *Communal dining and living areas in centre of building* • *Innovative resolution of building requirements, for example recessed fire doors*

Moorside
Durngate
Winchester
Hampshire SO23 8DU
Tel: 01962-854548
Fax: 01962-854811

Owner
St. John's Winchester Charity

Contact person for further information
Roger Battersby

Type of building
Residential home/nursing home

Architect
PRP Architects

Resident profile
Ambulant, with levels of confusion

DESCRIPTION OF BUILDING

Site context
Urban

Number of resident beds
23

Number of respite or assessment beds
3

Details of other overnight accommodation
One bedroom with en suite facilities that could be used as a guest bedroom for relatives of a resident or for staff sleepover in exceptional circumstances.

The approach to the entrance courtyard is similar in scale and character to the other buildings around the centre of Winchester.

Plan form

The plan takes the form of a T-shape with access via a lift at the central junction. Residents' bedrooms are provided in two clusters of eight bedrooms and one of seven. The three respite bedrooms are provided in the form of a mini-cluster.

Ancillary and service accommodation is located on the ground floor in the footprint of one of the first floor clusters.

Communal and shared space for residents

Each cluster takes the form of a large apartment with its own shared living room and dining room, kitchenette and assisted bathroom.

In addition there is a quiet room on each floor and a hobbies room and a hairdressing room on the ground floor.

A larger garden room doubles as a day centre for visitors and for use by residents.

Staff facilities

A nineteenth-century cottage adjoining the new home has been converted to provide staff facilities in the form of separate male and female changing and shower rooms, a staff rest room and a meeting/conference room with kitchenette and toilet facilities.

A nurses' station is provided on each floor within the home. Separate toilet facilities are also provided for kitchen and care staff within the home.

Office and administration space

A main office is located at the entrance/reception area with a door linking it to a reception/"shop" counter. A separate office with a small interleading store is provided for the head of home.

Service and ancillary spaces

A full central catering kitchen with related food and refuse storage facilities is located in a separate single storey wing. Other ancillary accommodation includes a central laundry, a sluice room on each floor, linen and cleaners' stores on each floor, a medical treatment room and other general storage areas.

What site constraints or external factors, such as existing buildings or local planning legislation, affected the form and planning of the building?

The limited size and difficult shape of the site. Urban location within the conservation area of a city of historical interest. Location on a prominent corner along a busy one-way traffic system. Archaeological remains. Access to site was limited to one point on northern boundary. Planning brief for prominent feature on corner.

Construction and external materials

Traditional load-bearing brickwork/blockwood walls, beam and block floors, trussed rafter roofs – plain clay tile roofs, stock facing bricks, recon stone cills, stained soft wood windows.

Type(s) of flooring

Impervious backed carpet to all residents' areas except en-suite WCs, assisted bathrooms, shared WCs and the kitchenettes which are non-slip vinyl sheet flooring. Ancillary accommodation floors are also finished in non-slip vinyl sheet flooring.

Internal finishes

Painted hardwall plaster, flush plasterboard ceilings - ceramic tiling to en suite areas and assisted bathrooms.

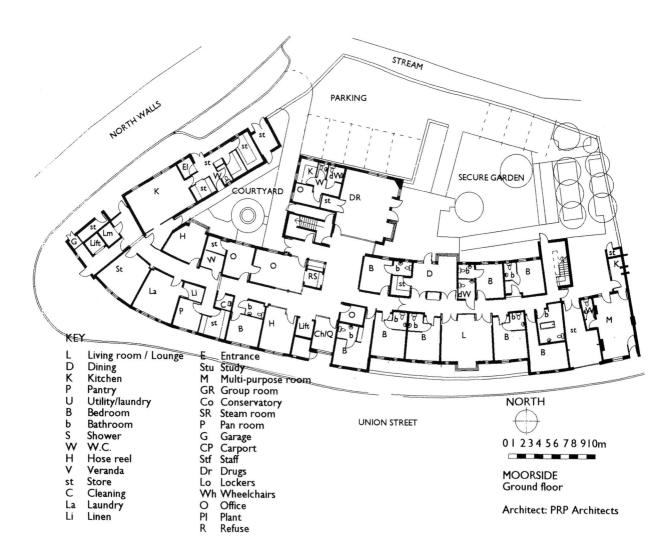

KEY

L	Living room / Lounge	E	Entrance
D	Dining	Stu	Study
K	Kitchen	M	Multi-purpose room
P	Pantry	GR	Group room
U	Utility/laundry	Co	Conservatory
B	Bedroom	SR	Steam room
b	Bathroom	P	Pan room
S	Shower	G	Garage
W	W.C.	CP	Carport
H	Hose reel	Stf	Staff
V	Veranda	Dr	Drugs
st	Store	Lo	Lockers
C	Cleaning	Wh	Wheelchairs
La	Laundry	O	Office
Li	Linen	Pl	Plant
		R	Refuse

UNION STREET

NORTH

0 1 2 3 4 5 6 7 8 9 10m

MOORSIDE
Ground floor

Architect: PRP Architects

Equipment

Three high-low baths, one shower cabinet, mobile hoists, grab rails, two macerators, two bed-pan washers, commercial and domestic laundry equipment, commercial catering equipment.

STAFFING

Management staff (per week full-time equivalents- FTE)

3 full time (matron, assistant matron and secretary)

Care staff (FTE)

7 (2 nurses, 5 care assistants)

Other staff (hours per week)

7 (1 laundry, 3 cleaners, 3 kitchen)

BUILDING STATISTICS

Site area within site boundaries

approx. 1,650m²

Ground floor area, i.e. "footprint"

approx. 880m²

Total floor area

1,697m²

Floor area of individual units of accommodation

17m²

Floor area of common living and dining rooms per group or cluster as appropriate (excluding separate circulation space and corridors)

50m²

Building cost including fixed equipment, hard and soft landscaping (but excluding loose furniture and fittings and professional fees)

£1,790,000

Details of elevations to the ring road showing the bay windows which allow living rooms wide views.

BUILDING DESIGN

The philosophy of care

To provide a supportive, domestic environment in which the hope, comfort, tranquillity and dignity of all residents can be maintained and to preserve and foster independence while understanding and supporting residents in the face of increasing frailty.

How was the philosophy expressed in the design of the building?

Internally by providing:

- Clusters or small groups of 7-8 bedrooms in the form of large flats/apartments;
- Each resident with their own room with en suite facilities and the opportunity to furnish their rooms with their own possessions;
- Each bedroom with its own "Front Door" set within a recess off the corridors;

Above, view of the ring road and adjoining fire station from one of the living rooms. Below, view from the dining room through to the living room, showing visual access. The glazed screens are a fire escape requirement. Fire doors fold unobtrusively into recesses.

Moorside's entrance courtyard has a water feature.

- A building layout that is simple in form, offers visual cues, colour codes and is therefore easy to find one's way around;
- A cluster layout which, although linear, is curved and thereby reduces the effective length of corridors. Centrally located open plan living and dining rooms on opposite sides of the corridor also reduce their effective length;
- Discretely-located service and ancillary accommodation away from areas which the residents would regard as "home";
- Staff rest, changing and meeting facilities discretely located in a separate but adjacent cottage where staff can effectively withdraw from the home;
- A demonstrably domestic environment in terms of the scale of the rooms, the way they are furnished and finished and the ways in which windows have been used;
- An environment that is well lit both in day time and at night. Choices for the residents in this urban location to overlook a busy street scene or a quiet garden, sit in a sunny room or a shaded one, enjoy the company of others or withdraw to their private rooms;
- A layout which while complying with restrictive legislation on fire fighting precautions, compartmentalisation and means of escape, is open plan, allows residents to wander (with extraneous doors held open in wall recesses) and facilitates their movement around the building;
- Easy access for the residents to a pleasant, quiet secure garden overlooking a stream;
- Quiet rooms where a disturbed resident can withdraw from the communal living within the cluster;
- A layout where visual accessibility has been maximised without compromising the residents' needs for privacy;
- A hierarchy of materials and finishes to assist residents by highlighting those aspects of the building, doors, etc., which are important to them and designing those aspects which are extraneous in terms of their immediate needs, i.e. staff, service and storage areas;
- An unobtrusive, flexible "wireless" warden call system.

For relatives and friends, by providing:
- A building in an urban community, of domestic scale and appearance which avoids the stigma of the institution;
- A pleasant, homely environment where they would be happy to spend time themselves and are therefore relaxed about leaving their loved ones in the care of others;
- An environment where they are made to feel welcome as visitors and are catered for in terms of meeting with their relatives in comfort and privacy.

Externally. By providing:
- An intimate tranquil entrance courtyard with water feature and aromatic plants.
- An easily accessible, quiet and secure garden, bordered by a stream, with a terrace for outdoor activities, and with areas of different character created along an easily-comprehensible, paved, circuit path which leads back to the terrace.
- A building of domestic scale and appearance constructed from local materials and laid out to address the busy street frontage in an urban location.

For Staff, by providing
- An environment that is clearly domestic and looks and feels like home to the residents so that the staff will respect it as such.
- Generous staff facilities in a location where they can effectively withdraw from the home.
- Convenient, well-equipped and well located staff and ancillary accommodation within the home to aid the process of care delivery, on the premise that well-supported and contented staff will provide better care support for residents.

Siting

The building has been sited to address the street on the long west boundary thereby:
- Maximising the development potential of the constricted and awkwardly shaped site;

- Avoiding the archaeological remains of the old city wall along the east boundary;
- Using the building as a barrier with which to create quiet courtyard gardens on the east side;
- Optimising the orientation of the rooms so that they will benefit from either morning or afternoon sunshine;
- Extending the terrace of houses to the south which faces directly onto the street.

Plan form

The principal accommodation is in the form of a "T" with the day centre/respite/garden wing in the short vertical leg. The linear block is curved to follow the street frontage. The service accommodation forms a further single-storey wing along the north boundary/street frontage.

This plan form allows access to each of the private clusters from the central junction point of the "T" where one of two lifts is located. This arrangement avoids through traffic within the clusters by care staff and other residents.

The central area acts as a transition zone between the public entrance reception area and the private cluster/apartments.

External character and appearance

Traditional construction and materials from local sources, chimneys and steeply pitched roofs reinforce the domestic scale and appearance along the long street frontage. In order to achieve the roof pitches the roof is split into two double pitched roofs with a central gutter. The plant rooms are concealed in the roof volume between the ridges.

Approach and entrance

Twin gables and a chimney provide a face to the home at the rear where access to the building is off the quieter street to the north.

A covered walkway leads one through an intimate entrance courtyard with a fountain and soft landscaping to the entrance door. Once inside the view out of the glazed entrance doors is contained by the courtyard to avoid attracting residents out into the dangers of the busy streets.

Signage and cueing

Statutory fire and means of escape signage has been minimised in terms of its extent and size whilst still complying with the regulations. Otherwise signage is minimised.

Residents' name cards are provided on their bedroom doors and there is scope for familiar objects to be applied to or adjacent to the doors for easy recognition. The layout, with the living and dining rooms open plan and on opposite sides of the corridor, provides easy visual cues to the residents.

The contrasting views from the building, i.e. busy street/quiet garden help in orientation. The residential clusters are colour-coded and the doors and ironmongery for residents and staff/service areas are differentiated.

Approach to colour schemes and interior design

Colour schemes in each residential cluster are different and soft furnishings have been carefully chosen to complement these colour ranges.

The use of carpet as a floor finish adds to the warmth and domestic atmosphere of all residents' areas. Light fittings have been chosen with reference to the residents' past and are therefore not overly modern in design.

Although the building is highly-serviced, flush plasterboard ceilings have been used throughout for their domestic appearance. Access panels have been provided where necessary for services. Doors which are not for general use by residents have been painted to match the surrounding wall colour.

Security provisions

Because of the potential dangers of the busy surrounding streets to residents, a security alarm system monitors all external doors and the garden gate. Doors to staff/service areas which might constitute a danger to residents are fitted with key pad entry controls and/or baffle handles.

Fire exit doors to the street are generally not in areas used by the residents. They are kept locked but released automatically in the event of the fire alarm being triggered.

Although the garden is completely enclosed by walls or fences these elements are softened by climbers and shrubs in the foreground and panels of railings which provide views beyond. Exit from the main entrance is controlled by a key pad.

The location of the main office and manager's office allow access and egress from the home to be monitored.

All windows are glazed with safety glass and fitted with restrictors.

Heating and/or air conditioning system

The heating is provided by central boilers in the roof plant room. It is a gas-fired, low pressure, hot water system with low surface temperature radiators.

Because of the noise generated by the traffic in the busy street an air supply and extract system has been ducted throughout the building. The air handling plant is also located in the roof plant room.

What technology is incorporated to assist in the care of people with dementia?

A "Wireless" CASS warden call system, which allows flexibility in terms of where the panel is located in a room, has been installed. Bedroom doors are monitored to alert staff to residents walking about at night.

There is an induction loop system for the hard of hearing in living dining areas and thermostatic blending valves to control water temperatures at taps.

To what extent were you able to achieve your intentions in the completed building?

To a large extent, particularly within the constraints of a small urban site. We have provided a very pleasant domestic environment for care delivery in an inner city location where the residents enjoy a range of choices, interesting views and involvement with city life.

There are inevitable compromises in choosing an inner city site for this client group – a single-storey building would in some respects be more appropriate and the linear plan dictated by the site makes dead-ends difficult to avoid.

What are the major hurdles which had to be overcome or prevented the intentions from being achieved?

- Planning requirements for a corner feature or tower are at odds with a domestic appearance.
- Stringent fire precaution legislation in a two-storey building provides a major obstacle to mobility.
- Security for residents in the face of the dangers presented by the urban traffic.
- Noise and pollution generated by the traffic.
- A very limited site for the amount of accommodation required by the brief.
- Accommodating a considerable amount of mechanical and electrical plant and services within the envelope of a domestic scale building.
- The width of the block is at odds with domestic scale.

Aspects of the building design worthy of replication

Moorside is very much a one-off in terms of its context and site constraints but the following aspects and principles of the design are worthy of replication:

- The linear cluster layouts with dual aspect living/dining areas which effectively "shorten" the corridors.
- Addressing the street with the building thereby returning to the traditional approach of creating quiet rear gardens.
- The curved layout which shortens the effect of corridors.
- The plan form which allows care to be delivered to residents' private areas from a central core.

To be avoided in the future

- A cluster size of three bedrooms (albeit for respite use) as it is uneconomical at staffing terms.
- The choice of site, which has proved to be high profile in terms of townscape.

Feedback

Moorside has now been occupied for two years and has been very well received by the owners, the staff and relatives and friends of the residents, many of whom have been very complimentary.

According to staff there has been a significant improvement in the demeanour and mobility of some residents who came to Moorside from long-stay mental institutions. There is a waiting list for residents who have applied for places and a day care centre is due to be opened shortly.

EDITORS' COMMENTS

The site and location of Moorside illustrates several aspects of building constraints in the UK. Winchester is a busy cathedral city with many historic buildings. Government planning policies encourage the development of sites within the boundaries of urban areas which are often of irregular shape and difficult to develop economically. The historic character of Winchester and the vernacular style of surrounding buildings influenced the planning and design of the new building. The materials are generally indigenous to the region and the arrangement of the building on the site creating an enclosed entrance courtyard and a small sheltered garden and the street elevations hard up to the back edge of the footpath retain the urban character of the city.

Moorside, which provides residential accommodation for 26 people and a day centre, is located within five minutes' walk of the city centre and is therefore rooted in the community. Shops and other facilities, swimming pool and bingo hall, are close by and residents can, with carers, easily visit them.

Although the simplicity and obvious functionality of a CADE-type solution appealed to the architects and to the clients, the shape of the site and the area available for building, together with doubts about the non-domestic or homely character of this approach which doesn't produce spaces of domestic room-like proportions, ruled such a solution out. The tight site led to a curving corridor plan which followed the boundary of the site and provided good visual access within each cluster.

The entrance is via a small courtyard which part of the building wraps around. On the ground floor the entrance area, a small foyer, gives on to the courtyard garden, the large sitting room which is a day centre and a small room, or chapel for contemplation and religious observance. The garden is a simple rectangular space with a path around the perimeter, open to the south and west, with a generous terrace sheltered by the two arms of the building and a pergola along one long side. These elements, with plantings and grass patches, provide variety and interest and a space that can be used for outside activities on warmer days.

The individual bedrooms on both sides of the corridor, each with en suite WC and washbasin but no shower, face south onto the small garden or north onto a busy road. The living and dining rooms are in the centre of each cluster on opposite sides of the corridor. It was the original intention that they should be open to the corridor but fire regulations made it necessary to provide glazed screens to isolate each space. However, with glazed doors held back in purpose designed recesses good visual access is maintained. The dining room contains a small "tea" kitchen or servery, all meals being prepared in a central kitchen and delivered to each cluster in heated trolleys.

Internally, the size and scale of the spaces and the detailed design and furnishing results in a building of domestic character. Externally the style of the building and the way it fits the site creates a timeless residential character which ensures that it in no way announces its essentially institutional purpose.

Moorside: Above, view of the gardens and terrace with pergola which will provide a shaded walk in summer. Below, view of the gardens from a living room which also provides a day centre facility.

Aldersgate Village

- Early pioneer in development of 'homely' nursing homes • Study, rather than nurses' stations • Choice of rooms for socialising or privacy • Strong redundant cueing • Strong relationship with surrounding neighbourhood • Use of, and relationship to, external spaces

Aldersgate Village Residential Nursing Units
160 O.G. Road
Felixtow
South Australia 5070
Tel: (+61) 2 9810 1362
Fax: (+61) 2 9810 1166

Owner
The Adelaide Central Mission
10 Pitt Street
Adelaide SA 5070

Contact person for further information
Stephen Alexander
Aldersgate
160 O.G. Road,
Felixtow SA 5070
or
Brian Kidd A.M.
42A Sulman Avenue
Salter Point WA 6152

Type of building
Residential home

Aldersgate Village: A view from the street showing the domestic style of the building.

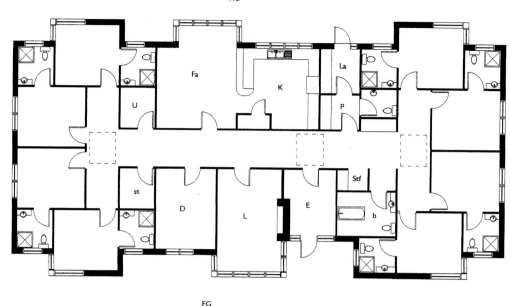

RG

FG

ALDERSGATE VILLAGE

Architect: Brian J Kidd

0 1 2 3 4 5 6 7 8 9 10m

KEY
E   Entrance
L   Formal Lounge
D   Formal Dining
K   Kitchen
Fa   Family room
La   Laundry
b   Bathroom
Stf Staff work area
Stu Study
P   Pan room
U   Clean Utility
st   Store
GS   Garden shed
Gz   Gazebo
CL   Covered link
FG   Front Garden
RG   Rear Garden
B   Bedroom
S   Shower
W   W.C.

Design for Dementia

92

Architect:
Stage 1, 1984. Brian J. Kidd in association with Brown Falconer Group. Stage 2, 1987. Brian J. Kidd.

Resident/client profile
Ambulant and non ambulant with levels of confusion and highly challenging behaviours. Stage 1 was originally a mixture of ambulant and bedfast residents, with three permanent wheelchair users. With increasing frailty levels, 80 per cent of the current residents are wheelchair users. Stage 2 caters for ambulant residents with levels of confusion.

DESCRIPTION OF BUILDING

Site context
The residential units are located on the corner of O.G. Road and Turner Street, in Felixtow, a residential suburb approximately 10 km from the centre of Adelaide. O.G. Road is a busy four-lane traffic route with a dividing median strip. The area opposite the site in O.G. Road is single residential housing.

Turner Street is a quiet side street, connecting to Briar Road and with a council swimming pool opposite. The three streets formed the boundaries of the Aldersgate Village, formerly a 25-acre property which was a self-contained retirement village for over 500 residents. This has since been redeveloped to provide private housing, leaving the aged care component as 59 nursing homes and 56 hostel residents.

Number of resident beds
The dementia specific component (Stage 2, 1987) provides for 27 ambulant nursing home residents, in three separate houses each for nine residents.

Stage 1 (1984) provides for 32 nursing home residents in two houses, each for 16 residents. Although not specifically intended to accommodate people with dementia, this was the first project to challenge the regulations. It produced a residential character nursing home using familiar domestic design and detailing, plus positive cueing and wayfinding techniques.

Number of respite or assessment beds
None

Details of other overnight accommodation
There are only bedrooms for residents. There are no staff bedrooms or guest rooms.

Plan form
Stage 1 consists of apartment modules of eight residents sharing a lounge room. The concept analogy is of a boarding house. The modules of eight were considered to be socially appropriate. Two groups of eight share common facilities such as dining room, study, bathrooms and utility rooms and form a 16-person residence. There are two of these residences, providing for a total of 32 residents.

Stage 2 consists of three individual houses, each for nine residents. Each house is fully self-contained, complete with lounge room, kitchen, family/dining room, bathroom, laundry and utility rooms. The houses were originally constructed with eight bedrooms each: a formal dining room did not get the use intended and has been converted into a ninth bedroom. Each house is fenced, with its own front garden and private rear garden.

The three units are physically separated, and each has its own street address and letter box. A covered way was originally intended, linking the buildings at the rear, but not constructed as it was feared this would negate the residential character. Subsequent experience has indicated that secure (but subtle) links are necessary for staff security.

Communal and shared spaces for residents

Each resident has a single room, which was in response to needs perceived by the Adelaide Central Mission at that time when shared rooms were the norm in nursing homes. Stage 1 was designed in the "boarding house" model with four bedrooms sharing a toilet and shower unit. Stage 2 provided an en suite facility to each bedroom.

All other facilities are shared. The residential units are designed in a desirable social grouping of modules of eight people. Each module shares a formal lounge room, each of which has a unique character.

In Stage 1, 16 people share a domestic kitchen, a dining room capable of accommodating 20 people, plus a small private dining room for six people (intended for family or special events).

In Stage 2, each household of eight people has a kitchen and family/dining room. A separate dining room for formal occasions was used insufficiently and later converted to a ninth bedroom in each house.

All other facilities are shared. Each household has a study, bathroom, visitor's toilet, laundry, clean and dirty utility rooms, cleaners' room and general storage, plus front and rear verandahs as an extension of living space. The formal front garden and the informal and securely fenced rear garden (with barbecue, garden sheds, lemon tree, aviaries, vegetable patches, etc.) are an essential element of the design.

Staff facilities

Each of the 16-person Stage 1 houses has a study. The nine-person Stage 2 houses each have a nook with a roll-top desk. Nearby buildings provide facilities for staff dining and changing rooms.

In the final site development, the staff facilities will be located in Forsyth House, the original family house dating back to the 1890s.

Office and administration space

Apart from the study and nook in each of the five houses, administrative offices for the whole site will be in Forsyth House, the community centre. Studies are provided in each house specific to the operation of each house.

Service and ancillary spaces

An existing central kitchen on the site originally prepared the main meals for the Stage 1, 16-person houses. However, all meals in the five houses are now prepared within each house.

Each house has its own laundry, clean and dirty utility. Centralised administration for the whole site is in a separate building.

What site constraints or external factors affected the form and planning of the building?

The site is on a corner, with a busy road on the western boundary, a small domestic road on the south, and existing buildings on the site to the east which defined the area for redevelopment.

However, the constraint was turned into an opportunity, allowing the houses to separate the remaining institutionalised buildings and interact with the houses in the surrounding residential community.

Construction and external materials

The character and construction of all buildings is of a domestic nature, with face brick external walls and tiled roofing (to four houses) and corrugated iron roof (to one house).

Covered ways have tiled roofing and timber lattice side enclosures, with brick paving.

Type(s) of flooring

Flooring is carpet, vinyl and mosaic tiles on a concrete slab. Floor finish to bathrooms, utility rooms, laundries and other wet areas are in non-slip 100mm x 100mm mosaic tiles. Kitchens and laundries are a non-slip vinyl sheeting. All other floors to bedrooms, lounge areas, dining room and passage ways are carpet.

Originally vinyl flooring was intended for the bedrooms (as was the usual practice in 1984). An in-house survey indicated that many spillages on floors were due to accidents (often by busy staff). Consequently, it was decided to use carpets as this is common in one's own home, and to embark on a dedicated maintenance and incontinence control programme.

Internal finishes.

All walls and ceilings internally are of plasterboard, with glazed ceramic tiles to bathrooms and over benches in other wet areas.

All corridors have a handrail on both sides which also assists in wall protection. External corners liable to damage have corner protection.

Equipment

The bathrooms in the two houses of Stage 1 each have a hydraulic bath, with a mechanical hoist. This bath was chosen primarily to ease the task of staff by minimising bending.

The houses in Stage 2 each have a bathroom, and the baths are each fixed peninsular type with a spa facility. All bathrooms are fully equipped with grab rails. Showers and basins used by residents have thermostatically controlled water supply.

A staff call system was not included originally in Stage 2, as it was considered that residents with dementia could not use the facility. A system was later installed under pressure from the licensing authority, but is virtually redundant. More sophisticated detection systems had not been developed at the time of building, and the small scale of the buildings appears to obviate this need. Exit doors all have security control devices.

STAFFING

Management staff

R/N	3.12 FTE	(118.37 hours)
DON	0.46 FTE	(17.39 hours)
Admin Assist	0.36 FTE	(13.73 hours)

Care staff

	14.97 FTE	(568.86 hours)

Other staff

(Gardening, maintenance etc.)	0.75 FTE

(FTE – per week full-time equivalents)

BUILDING STATISTICS

Site area within site boundaries
7,000m²

Ground floor area i.e. "footprint"
2,400m²

Total floor area
2,400m²

Floor area of individual units of accommodation

Stage 1: 12.5m² per bedroom
Each bathroom 12m² shared between four residents.

Stage 2: 14.0m² per bedroom
4.0m² per en suite (one to each bedroom)

Above, the kitchen, with a view into the back garden. Below, a typical corridor with access to individual rooms.

The secure rear garden with terrace and enclosing fence is an essential element of the design.

Floor area of common living and dining rooms per group or cluster as appropriate (excluding separate circulation space and corridors)

Stage 1:

Lounge room

32m² per 8 residents = 4m² per resident.

Dining room

40m² per 16 residents = 2.50m² per resident.

i.e. 6.50m² per resident.

Total = 6.50m² per resident.

Stage 2:

Formal lounge room 28m² per 8 residents = 3.5m² per resident.

Family dining room 24m² per 8 residents = 3.0m² per resident.

Total = 6.50m² per resident.

Building cost including fixed equipment, hard and soft landscaping (but excluding loose furniture and fittings and professional fees)

Stage 1

1984 Contract Price A$1,440,000 for 32 residents

(i.e. A$45,000 per bed).

Stage 2:

1987 Contract Price A$750,000 for 24 residents

(i.e. A$31,250 per bed).

NB. The cost difference was largely due to a change to smaller scale buildings using domestic construction techniques, and contractors specialising in residential construction.

BUILDING DESIGN

The philosophy of care

The philosophy of care is to provide a supportive environment in which the residents are empowered to participate in decisions affecting their lives. The philosophy of the design was to create an "enabling" environment which utilised the residual abilities of the residents. The design was to be of a familiar residential character, a simple and easy-to-read plan, era-appropriate, and with appropriate cues to assist the residents to relate to the environment and for easier orientation and wayfinding. The design caters for residents with mobility, sensory and cognitive losses in a positive way.

How was the philosophy expressed in the design of the building?

Internally. (*i*) The building has a simple plan for residents and evokes memories of homeliness. It is era-appropriate in decor, and reflects the character of the adjacent heritage building (Forsyth House), translating its bay windows, verandahs, stained and etched glazing, fireplaces or rich details in a contemporary manner. The houses were perhaps the first to introduce the gas log fireplaces, which are included as a conversation-gathering focus.

The lounge room for each eight people is placed to enable the users to view the front door or arrival area and to view activities inside. The kitchen is located centrally, being close to the front door and also able to supervise the back garden. The kitchen is of domestic character and useable by residents. Utility rooms are included but are discreetly located so as not to detract from the domestic character.

The plan is simple so as to minimise decision-making points (see signage and cueing).

(*ii*) The residential character of the design, with its familiarity and simple layout, was also intended to help get relatives and friends involved. The domestic kitchen can also be used by visitors to the homes.

A designated dining room for use by families was included but not utilised as residents and their families prefer to use the family/dining room and they have now been converted into a ninth bedroom in each house in Stage 2.

(iii) The building is functional for staff, who appreciate the pleasant domestic character. A study is included in lieu of the traditional nurses' station. It is located adjacent to the front entrance, allowing the staff subtle supervision in a pleasant environment combining a working environment with a relaxing lounge area.

Roll top desks were used, enabling private work to be locked away, as the rooms can be accessed by the residents. *Externally.* The buildings are domestic in scale and materials and are designed to blend into the adjacent residential context. They are perceived as another house in the street and thus are welcoming and friendly for residents, relatives and staff, as well as neighbours.

Siting

The new nursing home units were deliberately sited on the corner site in order to be recognised as part of the local residential community. The intention was to look outwardly to relate to the community, rather than to be introverted in the manner of the previous institution.

Plan form

The plan form for the Stage 1 houses is formal and symmetrical. Research indicated that a symmetrical plan is easier to navigate, particularly for people with cognitive deficits.

External character and appearance

The buildings appear as five homes in the community. The five houses all have a different appearance and presentation to the street. All external walls are face brickwork, with different colours to each building. Two houses have terracotta roof tiles, two have different coloured concrete roof tiles, and one has a colorbond corrugated galvanised iron roof. The intention was to look as if several owners and builders had developed the site.

Approach and entrance

Although Stage 1 presents to the street as houses, the entrances are inside the site and related to the grand arrival point in front of Forsyth House, the original residence on site.

The Stage 2 houses gained in confidence and each has a front door directly addressing either O.G. Road or Turner Street. The houses are identified by a postal number on the street frontage gatepost. Each house has a separate identity, and each has a front fence, front gate and letterbox, and a pathway leading directly to the front door, which is sheltered in each case by either a front verandah or a porch.

Approach to signage and cueing

The building has a minimum of written signs as the intention was for the architecture itself to impart clear messages of identification.

The houses in Stage 1 related directly with the grand presence of Forsyth House. Accordingly they are each identified by a beaten copper nameplate in the manner of large houses of past generations. One is named "Pomroy" (acknowledging a benefactor) and the other "Wisteria" (chosen by the residents and staff).

Stage 2 houses are simply identified by their street numbers e.g. Nos. 166 and 168 O.G. Road, and No. 1 Turner Street.

In line with social role valorisation, brass plaques honouring donors, or large external signs denoting an institution or special facility, were not considered. Such signs tend to stigmatise a project and would separate it from its residential neighbour.

The design tries to use the buildings themselves as a language. The front door has a bell and a distinctive stained or etched glass panel. The entrance hall is furnished with familiar elements such as wall hangings, bowls of flowers or a sideboard cabinet, a comfortable chair for people waiting to go

out and a telephone on a small table with a chair alongside.

Each house has a distinctive style and character, much in the manner of housing in the community. This then assists in identification (particularly helpful to a resident with wandering tendencies) and makes an event of a visit "next door".

All living rooms have a distinctive character. Each of the two houses in Stage 1 has two lounge rooms (one for each social group of eight people). Each of these is distinctive and easily recognisable, each with a unique ceiling profile, wall colours, light fittings, fireplace and mantelpiece and furniture.

The doors identify the use within the room. Stores and service (or staff areas) are plain, flush-panelled doors, usually painted in the wall colour. Bedroom doors have timber beading in a range of different panels to assist in personalisation. Doors into lounge rooms and dining areas (i.e. communal social spaces) are in glazed panels, to enable residents in a subtle (not goldfish bowl) manner to "see and be seen".

Cueing is a strong feature throughout the houses. A system of redundant cueing was incorporated, allowing for different personality types. For example, some of us respond primarily to visual information, others to tactile, others to light and shade, etc. At key decision points in the building several cues are provided (e.g. a flower box, skylight, artificial light fittings, and distinctive wall colouring).

Approach to colour schemes and interior design

Colour has been used as a major tool in assisting the residents to know and possess their own environment. Research indicated that older people perceive colours differently from other age groups. As we age, the lenses in our eyes tend to "yellow". Soft or pale colours are therefore disguised and not separately distinguishable. Consequently stronger colours and contrasts have been used. Each bedroom is personalised with a distinctive wall and trim colour. In communal areas, colour is again used positively to assist recognition and identification.

Reference was also included in the psychology of colour, as studies indicate that emotional reactions relate to specific colours.

Interior decor was selected to be era-appropriate. In acknowledgement of the reality that residents will have come from a variety of social backgrounds, localities and housing experiences, there are several different themes. The classical houses of Stage 1 have a formal and dignified theme. The three houses in Stage 2 all differ, one having Regency, one Federation and one in Alfresco style. Furniture had to be domestic, but robust and ergonomically appropriate.

Security provisions

Stage 1 does not have fencing, and is contained by thick shrubbery planting on the street boundary, and the trellis cladding of the covered ways elsewhere. Doors are not secured during daytime, although visitors are admitted after knocking on the front door.

Stage 2 houses each have a fenced in front and rear garden. The front fences are of flowering hedges, a type of fencing common in the neighbourhood. Each has a front gate and letterbox. Side and rear fences are of pine boarding 1.8 metres high and without horizontal rails as these would provide a foothold. The front doors have a manual combination lock, and other external doors are fitted with reed switches.

Heating and/or ventilation system or air conditioning system

Stage 1 has a centralised reverse-cycle air-conditioning system. Evaluation has found this system to be unsatisfactory, as there is no individual control to cater for varying needs. There is also conflict between the needs of staff and residents.

Stage 2 adopted a system allowing for individual preference. The lounge and family/dining areas are air conditioned, and the bedrooms have ceiling fans. The building has a hydronic heating system, with control to each room.

Technology used

There is little monitoring technology adopted in the buildings. One reason is that appropriate technology had not been developed or adopted at the time of design: the main reason is that it was considered that the small scale of the houses would mean that supervision and support would be on a very personal and intimate basis. Small numbers, small distances and a central focus around the kitchen and secure rear garden have resulted in little need for other devices.

Success in meeting intentions

Both stages were pioneers in the development of the "home-like" or "cluster" models and as such did not have precedents or prior evaluations from which to learn. The intention was to:
(i) Create an alternative approach to the previous "acute hospital model" of design and operation.
(ii) To design an enabling environment which encouraged residents to use their residual abilities to live as "normally" as possible. The buildings were to be familiar and comforting, utilising cues to assist in orientation and wayfinding.

The challenge in Stage 1 was to provide a viable alternative to previous nursing homes, challenging the existing regulations and showing the benefits of a homelike environment for residents, staff and relatives.

Stage 2 took this idea to the next stage and designed smaller house units which were able to be constructed at residential rather than commercial or industrial costs.

Major hurdles that had to be overcome or prevented the intentions from being achieved

There were several major hurdles to overcome.
- The need to challenge regulations for nursing home designs which resulted in plans similar to an acute hospital and a consequent similar method of operation.
- The insistence of some authorities that their task was purely to administer and enforce existing regulations and that they had no mandate to allow innovative thinking.
- The inability of some authorities to (initially) think laterally.
- The lack of precedents to support our submissions and alternative suggestions.
- The need to develop a strong case for our submission to answer the spirit of the regulations and to show that the intentions had other translations.
- The lack of availability of support from other organisations, as contemporary thinking in the aged care field was not at this stage in 1984-87. The notable exception was Aged Cottage Homes who at that time were exploring similar directions and encouraged the Adelaide Central Mission through discussion sharing and exploration of ideas.
- The need to change attitudes and work practices within the Adelaide Central Mission staff, as a new building form (resulting from a specific philosophic directional change) meant a major change in service delivery and care methods.

Aspects of the building design worthy of replication and also needing further development
- The domestic scale of eight or nine people;
- the familiarity of the house;
- the kitchen as a focus;
- the kitchen as an activity area;
- the secure back garden as a wandering space and activity space;
- the fireplace as a conversational focus;
- clear identification of bedroom doors;
- en suite to each bedroom;
- choice of communal areas (e.g. formal lounge, family/dining room, alcoves, bedroom, rear verandah);
- the use of distinctive colour and colour contrast;
- the use of natural light;
- the extensive use of cues for identification and assistance in orientation and wayfinding;

- clear visual interaction;
- a simple and non-labyrinthine plan;
- safety and security measures such as cut off controls to stoves, thermostatic controls to taps, grab rails, safety glass, etc. while allowing for sensible and calculated risk taking (e.g. gas flame fireplace, but with a safety mesh screen for protection).

The major lesson is that small, separate units must have fully enclosed linkages to the next house in order to give staff a feeling of security and in order to increase proper functioning and interaction between staff of the houses.

Feedback

Initial feedback was sufficiently positive to encourage development of the idea, the main evaluation being from observation, conversation and anecdotal evidence.

The residents settled into the new environment in surprisingly quick time. Most people appeared to be "at home" within a week, whereas previous experience indicated much longer times to settle in.

The residents' morale and self-image improved noticeably and their dressing habits improved noticeably in response to the dignity of the new environment.

One initial resident, who had become very dependent in the previous "dependency creating" environment, appeared to rejuvenate, becoming president of the residents' committee, displaying a real sense of pride and ownership in "her house" and walking with a stick or walking aid rather than being pushed around in a wheelchair as previously.

Approval was shown by friends and relations in that the frequency of their visits increased three to four-fold. They were now "proud" of the house in which their relative lived, whereas previously they had feelings of guilt and embarrassment.

The staff initially had to undergo major directional changes in work practices and the manner in which they related to the residents. Thinking had to change from "wards to bedrooms" and from "patients to residents". After some doubts, staff enthusiastically responded to the delights and relaxing atmosphere of the new "houses". Some openly said they now really enjoyed coming to the workplace, which was functional, yet pleasant and stimulating.

EDITORS' COMMENT

Aldersgate Residential Nursing Units hold a special place in the Australian experience of nursing home design. Stage 1 of the development (1984) overcame tremendous obstacles from regulatory authorities in what constituted a permissible environment for nursing care. At the same time the new building form, driven by changed philosophy of care, transformed attitudes and work practices of personal care staff.

Aldersgate's "homelike environment" is fundamental. While individuals many have very different views of what "home" looks like, Aldersgate's environment was and is consonant with the idea that "homeliness" infers "a place of one's domestic affection", a place where there is the ability and trust for affection to take place. (Peter Ireland, *Access in Dementia Design*, paper delivered in May 1996 at Dementia Design Conference, Sydney, Australia).

This domesticity is reflected externally by the orientation to the neighbourhood, including street addresses. Internally this domesticity is reflected in the simple non-labyrinthine plan, the inclusion of a study rather than a nurses' station, the kitchen as a focus and activity area, the fireplace as a conversational focus and a choice of rooms, apart from one's bedroom for socialising or for privacy .

ADARDS

● *Yard areas are very domestic* ● *Use of animals such as chickens and other birds*
● *More 'male' activities, such as washing and polishing the car* ● *Emphasis on natural light* ● *All weather walking* ● *Innovative design solution to night staffing*

The ADARDS Nursing Home
5 Bounty Street
Warrane
Tasmania 7018
Tel: (+61) 3 6244 7145
Fax: (+61) 3 6244 5787

Owner
ADARDS Nursing Home Inc

Managing Organisation
The Committee, ADARDS Nursing Home

Contact person for further information
Dr J.S.H. Tooth

Type of building
Residential home

Architect
David Hoffman

Resident/client profile
Ambulant, with highly challenging behaviours

DESCRIPTION OF BUILDING

Site context
Suburban

Number of resident beds
31

Number of respite or assessment beds
One

The ADARDS nursing home: A view of the buildings showing the steep site. Note the skylights which allow extensive use of natural light.

Design for Dementia

Outdoor seating with barbecue facilities helps encourage a homelike atmosphere.

Details of other overnight accommodation
One general purpose room which converts into a bedroom for relatives when they are assisting in the palliative care of a resident.

Plan form
There are four eight-bed houses – all with single bedrooms. The four houses are connected at the ends of the bedroom wings to a central area containing night nurses station, night lounge and administration areas.

Communal and shared spaces for residents
Each of the four houses has a kitchen, dining room, lounge room, verandah, laundry, two communal toilets and assisted bathroom. There is also a large general purpose room which is central to the four houses and used by all residents.

Staff facilities
In each house there is a staff toilet and hand basin. In the central area there is a staff tea room, locker room, shower room, toilet, nurses' station and treatment room.

Office and administration space
Offices for receptionist, director of nursing and one for interviewing. There is also a clinical administrative area, waiting area, stationery store, general purpose room.

Service and ancillary spaces
In each of the four houses are a kitchen, laundry, assisted bathroom, two small storage areas. In the central area there is a sluice/pan room, a food store, occupational therapy store and a treatment room.

What site constraints or external factors, such as existing buildings or local planning legislation, affected the form and planning of the building?
Steepness of site, narrowness of site, access to site.

Construction and external materials
Slab on ground floors, brick veneer walls, and timber roof trusses. Brick, aluminium windows and colorbond steel roofing.

Type(s) of flooring
Flotex in living rooms, dining rooms and corridors. Safety vinyl in bedrooms, en suites, kitchens, bathrooms, communal toilets, shower rooms and laundries. Concrete to verandahs.

Internal finishes
Medium density fibre board to corridor walls below handrails, plasterboard to walls and ceilings generally and Villaboard to en suites and shower rooms. Noise-stop board, acoustic batts to walls, double glazing, baffled vent to one sound-proofed bedroom.

Equipment
Parker bath, grab rails, steriliser, cleaner's sinks, slop hopper.

STAFFING

Management staff
1.75 per week full-time equivalents—FTE
Care staff
25.2 FTE
Other staff
4.87 FTE

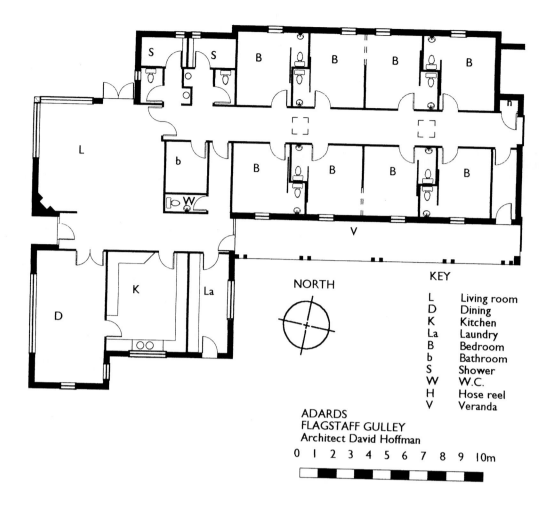

KEY
L — Living room
D — Dining
K — Kitchen
La — Laundry
B — Bedroom
b — Bathroom
S — Shower
W — W.C.
H — Hose reel
V — Veranda

NORTH

ADARDS
FLAGSTAFF GULLEY
Architect David Hoffman
0 1 2 3 4 5 6 7 8 9 10m

BUILDING STATISTICS

Site area within site boundaries
6,325m²

Ground floor area i.e. "footprint"
1,686m²

Total floor area
1,686m²

Floor area of individual units of accommodation
14.5m²

Floor area of common living and dining rooms per group or cluster as appropriate (excluding separate circulation space and corridors)
80m²

Building cost including fixed equipment, hard and soft landscaping (but excluding loose furniture and fittings and professional fees)
A$1,600,000

BUILDING DESIGN

The philosophy of care

To provide care for ambulant people with dementia and the most difficult and challenging behaviours in small homelike environments which have a warm and welcoming ambience and ensure a reduction in frustration of residents and staff. This environment to provide "normal" household activities for residents and be supportive for them as well as for relatives and staff. Maximum cost-efficiency has been achieved.

How was the philosophy expressed in the design of the building?

Internally. For residents: By using a design which converts the four houses from autonomous operation by day to a 32-bed facility at night, sufficient staff efficiencies have occurred to enable the houses to accommodate as few as eight residents each. With this relatively small number a homelike atmosphere was able to be achieved.

By providing a kitchen, in which all meals are cooked, in the centre of each house in order to provide appropriate food smells. By providing large living rooms with imitation log-fires and dining rooms next to the kitchens.

By providing single bedrooms with built-in wardrobes and en suites that can be seen from the bedroom.

By providing simple corridor paths for walking or wandering that connect with a verandah and provide a change in environment. By providing features which reduce frustration for residents. These include disguised doors leading to places where residents should not have access.

For relatives and friends: By providing an environment for their loved ones that looks and feels like a home. The dining rooms and living rooms in each house are large enough for relatives to visit at all hours and share meals with the resident. For staff: By providing an environment that looks and feels like home whilst also being secure so that staff can be relaxed and unhurried.

By providing staff toilets in each house with disguised access and central staff facilities which include a tea room, locker room and shower room.

By connecting the bedroom wings so that night staff have security and ease of vision into bedroom corridors. There are short distances to all bedrooms, a comfortable central lounge area where residents not sleeping can stay without disrupting other residents and electronic sensors to alert staff when a resident is out of bed.

By providing features that reduce staff frustration, including disguised wardrobes in the bedrooms where folded clothes can be kept and faecal drains under the en suite showers.

By designing an environment that reduces anxiety and frustration in residents by avoidance of dead-end corridors and locked doors.

Externally: For residents: By having garden areas accessible from living areas with paths that lead residents back again to the house.

By the provision of familiar fencing, clothes hoists, barbecues, outdoor seating, a chicken run, aviary and an old car for washing and polishing as well as flower and vegetable beds – all providing a generally domestic feeling.

By providing secure containment, which is not obvious, and disguised exit doors.

For relatives and friends: By providing the familiar front and back garden spaces so that homeliness persists inside and out.

By having access for visitors to living areas along verandahs passing by attractive gardens. By providing outdoor areas where relatives feel that their loved ones are safe.

For staff: By providing generally good views of garden spaces. By enhancing the feeling of home through the character of the external spaces.

By having safe outdoor areas which also ensure secure containment of residents.

Siting

The four houses are grouped around and connected to a central area.

The site, which had a substantial cross fall, has been cut and filled to provide a single floor level and a generally level site.

The houses sit square to adjacent roadways, amongst suburban houses and near to a primary school.

Plan form

The plan form is cross-shaped, with bedroom corridors extending to the central administration area. The living areas are at the end of the bedroom corridors away from the central area.

External character and appearance

The external character and appearance is as domestic and residential as the houses in the adjoining neighbourhood. The houses are different in appearance from each other to match the diversity found in the nearby suburbs.

Approach and entrance

The approach is through suburbs and then via a lane alongside a car park screened by a fence of large lattice. The entry is under a large carport to the reception office or to pairs of entry doors that lead to the houses either side of the reception area.

Signage and cueing

There is no signage other than names on doors and cueing is by the visibility of familiar items. Dressing gowns on ends of wardrobes, visible from the bedroom corridors, are remarkably successful in assisting residents to identify their bedrooms. Toilet doors and hand basins are visible from corridors and the simplicity of the plan form makes wayfinding easy.

Colour schemes and interior design

Colour schemes in each house are different to enhance diversity and to give prospective residents' relatives a sense of each house being special and different.

The colours are light and bright and each bedroom and living area is different in order to assist residents in wayfinding. In corridors a darker tone below handrails gives a stabilising feel and takes marking better than the lighter colours above. Colours are not unusual for the spaces they are used in. Warmer colours are used more than cooler ones.

The approach to interior design was to create as homely and

homelike environment as possible with furniture, furnishings and ornaments as familiar and functional as could be.

Carpet is Flotex for functional reasons and for appearance. The pattern used is one that is floral in appearance, not visually disturbing and domestic in character.

Security provisions

Doors from houses to garden areas have electronic release latches connected to a fire alarm system. During the day these doors are not locked.

Doors from the bedroom wings to the central area are closed during the day with magnetic locks and held open at night with magnetic hold-open devices.

Doors used during the day for visitors and staff access to the houses are unlocked on entry but from the house side they are locked, without handles and camouflaged to resemble the wall. Residents do not identify them as doors and there is no locked handle to frustrate them.

There is a security fence of "tennis court" wire around the perimeter and this will soon be covered by climbing plants.

Fences between the garden areas have rails with sloping tops to discourage footholds on one side and flush palings on the other. Through changes in ground level, some public external fences appear of normal height on the outside but are actually higher on the inside.

The ability of night staff to see all 32 bedroom doors from their central station provides security for staff and residents at night.

Heating and/or ventilation system or air conditioning system

In living areas there is radiant ceiling heating whilst in bedrooms, en suites and corridors, floor heating is used. In the living rooms an imitation log fire is provided in fireplaces.

Ventilation is by exhaust fans from en suites, kitchens, bathrooms and laundries, either direct to the outside or into the ventilated roof space. General room ventilation is natural through windows.

Technology used

There are motion detectors in each bedroom which alert the night nurse in the centre via a mimic panel when the resident is out of bed.

The controls of kitchen stoves are isolated by keyed switches away from the stoves themselves. There are isolation valves on hot and cold water supplies and thermostatic control of the temperature of hot water.

Success in meeting intentions

We believe we have succeeded completely. We have provided a facility of four domestic-style houses, each with a warm and friendly ambience, which has not only proved quite capable of accommodating those ambulant residents with dementia and the most disturbed behaviours but has also contributed to the diminution of disturbed behaviour. It has also been at least as cost-effective as we had hoped.

Major hurdles that had to be overcome or prevented the intentions from being achieved.

Site constraints of width of block.

Aspects of the building design worthy of replication?

- The concept of changing from small houses by day to a 32 bed "ward" by night has meant very considerable saving of expensive night staff. Thus we have been able to have small houses and to put more staff on in the day so that more activity programmes can be achieved. As a result the residents sleep better at night. It is hard to understand why no other organisation has adopted this design concept until this year.
- Night lounge in central area for residents who are up at night.

Residents enjoy special features such as the chicken coops (above) and an old car in the garden area.

Above, the working kitchen for an eight-bedroomed house. Below, en suite facilities off a resident's bedroom.

- The camouflaged doors. Three doors in each house are camouflaged or disguised. They are the exit doors to the central area, the staff toilet and the assisted bathroom. Each of these doors is painted to resemble the wall, has no handle, only an unobtrusive keyhole. We believe that every door with a handle must be unlocked and so have eliminated the frustration of residents rattling on locked doors.
- The homeliness and true domestic character of the separate houses.
- Functioning kitchens with preparation of food in each house.
- Living room, dining room and kitchen arrangement for ease of resident movement and supervision by staff.
- The cueing of bedrooms by hanging dressing gowns next to the open door appears to be considerably more effective in enabling residents to find their bedrooms than the alternatives of "colour-coding", photographs or window boxes.
- Locked, disguised parts of wardrobes and unlocked "rummageable" parts.
- The arrangement of bedroom corridors, passages to verandahs and verandahs for walking about in all weathers and also for wandering.
- Plan arrangement that avoids "dead-ends" in corridors.
- The use of natural light.
- The use of chickens, birds, dogs and cats in the secure house gardens. Chickens are particularly helpful in the context of the culture of Tasmania as many of the residents used to keep them. Collecting the eggs or simply watching the fowls as they move around appears to be a fulfilling occupation for residents.
- The use of an old car in the grounds. In any dementia unit there are usually fewer activities available for older men than for older women. Some men take great delight in washing and polishing the car.

To be avoided in future

Commercial laundries in each house. We started with domestic laundries in each house for the washing of small personal items but converted them so that they could launder the soaker pads from the beds. We now feel that it would be better to have a central laundry for these articles.

Feedback

Our resident group has progressed too far in the course of the disorder to make a verbal expression relevant. However the non-verbal language indicates that the majority are content and much of the time happy in the facility.

We have had numerous verbal and written messages of approval of this facility from friends and relatives. The following quotes are typical:

"It is the atmosphere of this place that is so wonderful. The design has made it feel like home whilst making sure that my husband is safe."

"To be able to wander freely from their bedroom through the lounge and dining room past the kitchen with its familiar smells and out into the garden through unlocked doors helps to lessen the feeling of confusion and gives them a sense of peace and security."

Generally the staff have been most appreciative of the overall design and the design features and there have been many favourable comments. The fact that there has not been one case of staff burn-out in five years may support this.

One Registered Nurse wrote the following on her retirement: "In a few words, the ADARDS Nursing Home provides an ideal (may I say perfect!) home and environment to care for people with dementia.

"There are many specific, unique features which provide great assistance to all staff members who administer this care. I was particularly appreciative of the well-planned en suite bathrooms attached to all bedrooms which provide privacy for each resident and easy access for staff to the resident's belongings for washing, dressing and grooming; the 'rummage' wardrobe for each resident which gives them the independence and freedom to 'potter' amongst their personal items without dislodging their good clothes.

"It was helpful from the nursing point of view to know that our residents could wander safely without danger. The many unlocked doors within each house and leading outside for residents to use provides a sense of freedom and not restriction and I am sure this reduces agitation and disturbance. After years of nursing in other facilities it was also so nice not to have residents knocking on locked exit doors. The camouflage of these was generally most effective.

"But I suppose that it was the homeliness of the place that made for so much contentment of residents and happiness of the staff. The cats, dogs, birds and chickens, vegetable and flower gardens all contributed to a relaxed atmosphere, while the domestic activities in the laundry and kitchen made us all feel at home. There is something very special about the smell of home cooking."

EDITORS' COMMENT

ADARDS has addressed the financial and staffing challenges of having four small, simple cottages of eight residents by opening the connecting doors at night so that fewer staff are required at night and more are at work during the active day hours.

The yard areas, which have chickens, birds, dogs and cats in the secure house gardens, have proved to be very beneficial as many residents in previous houses used to keep animals. Collecting eggs or simply watching the fowls has proved beneficial.

Daily living activities for men are very important and ADARDS has more "male" activities occurring in the yard, such as washing and polishing the car.

Other excellent features are the emphasis on natural light, including extensive use of skylights, and the arrangements which allow all-weather walking.

Woodlands

Reasons for selection

● *Direct access to garden area from ground and first floor* ● *Attractive sheltered external spaces and landscaping* ● *Good daylighting in circulation areas* ● *Domestic atmosphere in living and dining rooms* ● *Good views over landscaped courtyard*

Woodlands Nursing Home
Renfrew Road
London SE11
Tel: 0171 793 0067
Fax: 0171 793 9589

Owner
Lambeth Healthcare (NHS) Trust

Contact person for further information
Carl von Buen

Type of building
Residential home

Architect
Penoyre & Prasad Architects
(Project architect – Stephen Coveman)

Resident/client profile
Ambulant, with levels of confusion

DESCRIPTION OF BUILDING

Site context
Urban, on an old hospital site

Number of resident beds
36

Number of respite or assessment beds
4

Details of other overnight accommodation
One guest room – though currently used as an office

Plan form
Four "houses" of 10 persons.

Communal and shared spaces for residents
Each of the "houses" has a sitting room which can be opened into the dining room and a separate quiet room.

Staff facilities
A staff base in each "house" plus admin, clinic and reception adjacent to main entrance.

Office and administration space
Home manager's office – 14m²
Reception/administrator – 12m²

Service and ancillary spaces
Each "house" has an assisted bathroom, domestic bathroom, dirty utility room.

There is a central kitchen – though main meals are brought in. There is a launderette for clients' clothes.

What site constraints or external factors, such as existing buildings or local planning legislation, affected the form and planning of the building?
Proximity to neighbours/potential for being overlooked and overshadowed by an adjoining tall building (water tower).

Construction and external materials
Externally insulated/rendered blockwork with concrete floor slabs – brick plinth and profiled aluminium roof – painted soft wood windows.

Type(s) of flooring
Quarry tile to entrance. Carpet generally and wood block to dining areas. Vinyl to bathrooms.

Internal finishes
Walls and ceilings mostly plastered and painted. Bedrooms and living/dining areas have picture rail.

Equipment
Assisted baths – Parker & Madison (elevating). Dirty utility – Sluicemaster macerator. Domestic baths – Parker Gold.

STAFFING

Management staff
1.5 FTE
Care staff
(Over a typical 24hrs) 5 primary nurses and 21 care assistants
Other staff
4.4 FTE (0.5 activity organiser, 1.0 administration, 0.5 driver/handyperson, 2.0 kitchen. 0.4 cleaning)

BUILDING STATISTICS

Site area within site boundaries
4200m²

Ground floor area i.e. "footprint"
790m²

Total floor area
1500m²

Floor area of individual units of accommodation
Bedrooms are 11.1m² including wardrobe.

Floor area of common living and dining rooms per group or cluster as appropriate (excluding separate circulation space and corridors)
Living 18.5m², dining 16m², quiet room 10m²

Woodlands: Looking towards the entrance from the central courtyard.

Colourful effect on a staircase landing.

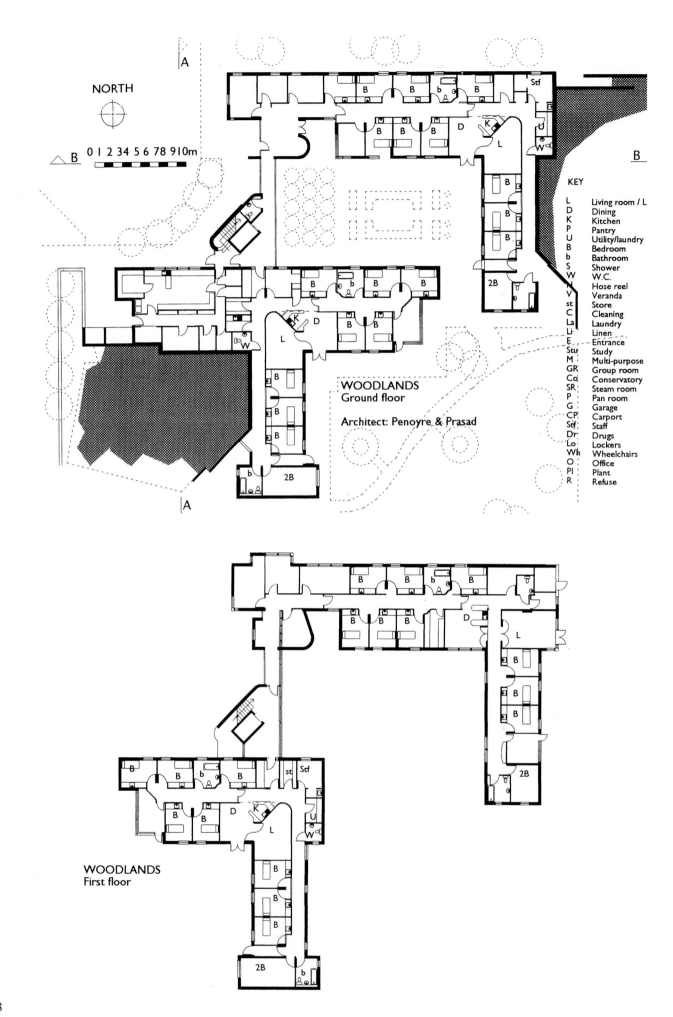

NORTH

0 1 2 34 5 6 78 910m

WOODLANDS
Ground floor

Architect: Penoyre & Prasad

KEY

L D	Living room / L
D	Dining
K	Kitchen
P	Pantry
U	Utility/laundry
B	Bedroom
b	Bathroom
S	Shower
W	W.C.
Hr	Hose reel
V	Veranda
st	Store
C	Cleaning
La	Laundry
Li	Linen
E	Entrance
Stu	Study
M	Multi-purpose
GR	Group room
Co	Conservatory
SR	Steam room
P	Pan room
G	Garage
CP	Carport
Stf	Staff
Dr	Drugs
Lo	Lockers
Wh	Wheelchairs
O	Office
Pl	Plant
R	Refuse

WOODLANDS
First floor

Building cost including fixed equipment, hard and soft landscaping (but excluding loose furniture and fittings and professional fees)
£1,500,000 (tendered 1993)

BUILDING DESIGN

The philosophy of care
To provide a comprehensive range of high quality, locally accessible health services, that offer equity of access and will support or maximise possibilities for "independent living" within the community.

How was the philosophy expressed in the design of the building?
Internally
For residents: maximum freedom of movement within a secure environment within building and through garden.
For friends and relatives: Openness of access, welcoming environment.
For staff: Good quality working environment
Externally
For residents: The gardens are integrated with the internal plans – comments as above.
For friends and relatives: High quality environment indicates value given to their relatives.
For staff: Good quality working environment.

Siting
The building is sited to ensure appropriate privacy to the residents and neighbours. Siting was further arranged to maximise sunny rooms, circulation and gardens and to provide variety of space and outlook.

Plan form
The 40 bedspaces are provided in four "houses" of 10 persons. Each house is "L" shaped in plan with a secure garden nestling in the crook of the "L".

External character and appearance
The external walls are of "honey" coloured render on a brick plinth with profiled aluminium roof sheeting.

Approach and entrance
The approach from the old hospital gates is clearly indicated by new paving. The entrance is under a canopy into a glazed gallery allowing glimpses into the central garden.

Approach to signage and cueing
This was procured separately by the client with no input from the design team (unfortunately).

Approach to colour schemes and interior design
Aim to aid orientation while stimulating the senses through different qualities of light, space, colour and acoustic treatment. Surfaces, such as handrails, are of different textures and there are niches for placing fragrances.

Security provisions
The front door has a coded door lock. Other boundaries are provided with close-boarded trellis (to prevent break-ins).

Heating and/or ventilation system or air conditioning system
Gas-fired central heating (wet system) with low surface temperature radiators.

Technology used
Call system and domestic equipment.

Success in meeting intentions
The design aims were to a large extent achieved. Where diffi-

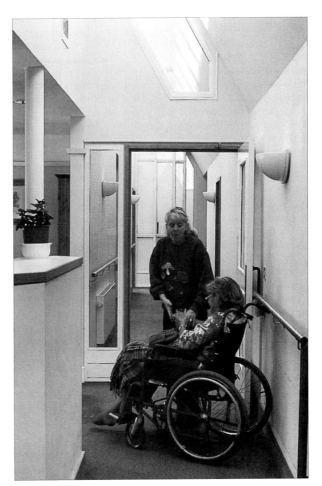

A corridor in one of the houses.

culties were encountered it was due to changes in brief and service provision during or after detailed design.

Major hurdles that had to be overcome or prevented the intentions from being achieved
A major hurdle is to meet the users of the building during design development – the client was helpful but a large corporate client may not be used to the extent of consultation we aim to carry out.

Aspects of the building design worthy of replication?
Light pleasant circulation, direct access to gardens for all residents, variety of spaces.
To be avoided in the future?
Lack of close communication between interior designers (signs, curtains, soft furnishings, etc.) and architects.

Feedback
Feedback has been circumstantial. No systematic evaluation has taken place.

EDITORS' COMMENT
Woodlands makes imaginative use of a redundant hospital site in an inner London suburb. The entrance to the building is, however, remote and the absence of surrounding residential development suggests an institutional use.

The entrance, viewed from the parking area in front, is immediately attractive due to the choice of materials, the use of colour and the large areas of glass. The entrance foyer has a domestic scale but is part of a glazed link between the two ground floor clusters. This allows views over the approach to the building and into the courtyard around which the building is planned from ground and first floor levels. The architects envisaged this space as an outside space, reflected in the ceramic tile floor and the large glazed sliding doors linking the outside spaces and the inside of the building. The management of the building have seen the space differently and provided full length curtains and generous pelmets in a large floral print which creates more the character of a Victorian conservatory. This ability to design spaces which can happily accept a variety of internal fittings and furniture is central to creating a homely and truly domestic environment.

The residential clusters, each with 10 single rooms, are L-shaped and have a dining space and small kitchen open to the corridor and a more enclosed living room with a fireplace feature. All the dining rooms have direct access to their own garden area sheltered by the arms of the L-shaped clusters. This is possible in a two-storey building because the clusters combine single-banked and double-banked corridors and by having the corridor on one side of the building at ground level and on the other on the first floor.

The corridor plans do not provide good visual access and the individual rooms are small, 11.1m² with only a wash basin in each room and no en suite facilities.

Meals are cooked in a central kitchen and delivered to each cluster in heated trolleys. The trolleys are large and are beginning to damage door frames and corners. The building is compactly planned and there is a pleasant contrast between the spaces within the clusters and the shared spaces connecting them. The use of a split-level roof, producing what North Americans call "cathedral ceilings", allows daylight and sunlight into the corridors of two of the clusters. It produces a pleasant effect, but creates a far from domestic character.

Above, communal spaces – a dining room in one of the houses. Below, a view from a garden towards the quiet room of another house.

Anton Pieckhofje

Anton Pieckhofje
Andsstraat 1
2034 Ml Haarlem
Tel: (+31) 23 566983
Fax: (+31) 23 566983

Owner
Woningrouwvereriging
"De Vonk"
Amerikaweg 10
2045 RA Haarlem
Tel: (+31) 23 5436300

Contact person for further information
Dr N. de Boer

Verpleeghuis Overspaarne
Beerhaavelaan 50
2035 RC Haarlem
Tel: (+31) 23 5339108
Fax: (+31) 23 5351744

Type of building
Care and living facility for elderly with dementia.

Architect
Frans v/o Werf BV
Voorschoterlaan 93
3662 KK Rotterdam
Tel: (+31) 10 4331738

Anton Pieckhofje: A view of the entrance and surrounding housing.

KEY
L   Living room / Lounge
D   Dining
K   Kitchen
P   Pantry
U   Utility/laundry
B   Bedroom
b   Bathroom
S   Shower
W   W.C.
H   Hose reel
V   Veranda
st Store
C   Cleaning
La Laundry
Li Linen
E   Entrance
Stu Study
M   Multi-purpose room
GR Group room
Co Conservatory
SR Steam room
P   Pan room
G   Garage
CP Carport
Stf Staff
Dr Drugs
Lo Lockers
Wh Wheelchairs
O   Office
Pl Plant
R   Refuse

ANTON PIECKHOFJE
Architect: Frans v/o Werf BV

01 234 5678 910m

NORTH

Resident/client profile
Ambulant and non-ambulant with challenging behaviours and high levels of confusion.

DESCRIPTION OF BUILDING

Site context
In the middle of the new Romolenpolder housing estate on the edge of the city.

Number of resident beds
36

Number of respite or assessment beds
None

Details of other overnight accommodation
Each house has one guest room (six in total)

Plan form
Six groups

Communal and shared spaces for residents
The building is like the traditional Hofje in Haarlem, built around a central garden.

Staff facilities
None. However the guest rooms and one other room are generally used by staff.

Office and administration space
Office for the whole complex is used by the co-ordinator.

Service and ancillary spaces
Glazed ambulatory around garden with sitting areas. Office, storage and meeting room.

What site constraints or external factors, such as existing buildings or local planning legislation, affected the form and planning of the building?
Practical reasons only. The town government decided on the building site's size and form.

Construction and external materials
Brick and concrete construction, grey sand lime bricks and white painted windows.

Type(s) of flooring
Domestic floor finishes in flats.

Internal finishes
Domestic finishes, plaster walls and ceilings.

STAFFING

Management staff
1.04 FTE
Care staff
33.34 FTE
Other staff
2.2 FTE

BUILDING STATISTICS

Site area within site boundaries
1,950m²

Ground floor area i.e. "footprint"
1,263m²

Total floor area
1,263m²

Floor area of individual units of accommodation
11.1-14.6m²

Floor area of common living and dining rooms per group or cluster as appropriate (excluding separate circulation space and corridors)
66.42m²

Building cost including fixed equipment, hard and soft landscaping (but excluding loose furniture and fittings and professional fees)
Not available.

BUILDING DESIGN

The philosophy of care

This experimental form of care for elderly people with dementia aims at providing care which resembles the home setting as much as possible. The concept of care for this group of people is meant to provide an environment in which people go on living much as they previously did in their own home: in a small-scale setting which resemble a family situation.

Six living units are built as ordinary houses of which the front doors open to a circular communal corridor with a garden in the middle. In each house six elderly people live together; each has a separate room of her or his own, and most daily living takes place in a communal sitting room. All "ordinary household functions" are performed in the house: cooking, eating, entertainment, etc.

Care is provided by a small set of professionals, preferably with help from the family; medical care is provided by a local family practitioner.

The general purpose is first and foremost to provide a high and non-institutional quality of life and care at no higher expenditure than the usual forms of care for this group.

How was this philosophy expressed in the design of the building?

Normal houses instead of an institutional appearance. A round courtyard for freedom of movement.

Siting

Surrounded by roads and footpaths. Children's play area and river adjoining.

Plan form

Ground floor flats planned around central courtyard, family flats at first floor level.

External character and appearance

(See *Editors' Comments*)

Approach and entrance

Double doors with canopy cover into entrance hall and ambulatory around central courtyard.

Approach to signage and cueing

No signage or cueing except for fire exits and fire alarm.

Approach to colour schemes and interior design

Choice of the architect.

Security provisions

There is an electronic lock, opened by a code, on the one door to the outside of the building.

An aerial view shows the central courtyard around which the residential accommodation is arranged.

Above, the ambulatory and flat entrances arranged around the central courtyard. Below left, entrance to a typical flat with kitchen window opening onto ambulatory. Right, a bedroom window looking out onto the ambulatory.

A shared sitting area off the ambulatory overlooking the central courtyard gardens.

Heating and/or ventilation system or air conditioning system
Central heating and ventilation system for each unit.

Technology used
Intercom, activated by sound, in each bedroom. This is used only at night.

Success in meeting intentions
We believe that we have succeeded one hundred per cent.

Major hurdles that had to be overcome or prevented the intentions from being achieved
Formal regulations on healthcare. Financial problems.

Aspects of the building design worthy of replication?
The total concept
To be avoided in the future?
More storage rooms should have been provided.

Feedback
Feedback from staff, friends and relatives has been very positive. An evaluation study commented that the project was "highly successful in providing a high quality of person-centred care in a situation resembling an ordinary household far more than most institutions". Families of inmates and personnel alike speak of a "difference between heaven and hell" in comparing this new form with more traditional ones.

EDITORS' COMMENTS
Anton Pieckhofje, named after a popular local painter, is really embedded in the local community. Houses adjoin it on two sides and there is a children's play area outside the entrance. Six flats, each for six people, are planned around a central courtyard linked by a glazed ambulatory which incorporates conservatory-like sitting areas. On the first floor are small flats for normal residential use.

It is a modern interpretation of the traditional "Hofje" or almshouses for which Haarlem is well known and which are also arranged around a central garden.

There is great emphasis on normality at Anton Pieckhofje. The shared facilities are minimal. Apart from the sitting areas around the courtyard there is a small meeting-cum-staff room and a manager's office. Each flat is run as a separate home and is largely autonomous. Residents help choose the food for their own meals and assist as far as they are able with preparing food and other domestic chores. There is no "cueing" because this destroys "normality" – it isn't what you would expect to have in your own home.

The flats, apart from the fact that each is for six people accommodated in six separate bedrooms, have no special distinguishing features. There is a small entrance hall with a cloakroom off, a generous living room with a modest open plan kitchen and a short, double-banked corridor which leads to the bedrooms and a large shared shower room. The areas of individual rooms, without en suite facilities, are adequate, similar to Woodlands. Total floor area per person is low compared with other buildings illustrated.

The building is built of grey sand lime brick and concrete and has a certain stark quality, but this is something found in many contemporary Dutch buildings. The generous windows to the living rooms of each flat, with decorative blinds or curtains and resplendent with indoor plants, all look outwards towards the surrounding streets and houses. Half the bedrooms and all the kitchens have their windows looking on to the ambulatory around the courtyard.

The ambulatory has fair faced brick walls and a continuous low level concrete cill around the courtyard with a grey tile and terrazo floor. The interiors of the flats have the usual domestic finishes – they are "normal".

Design for Dementia

115

Kinross Hostel

- *Well integrated into the surrounding community* • *Homely and comfortable lounge rooms* • *Interior decor* • *Separate activities room* • *Good access to garden areas* • *Administration building separate from cottages*

Kinross Hostel
71 Kinross Drive
Kinross
Western Australia 6028
Tel: (+61) 2 9383 1088
Fax: (+61) 2 9381 4559

Owner
Anglican Homes (Incorporated)

Contact person for further information
Mr Peter McHale, Manager

Type of building
Residential home (segregated hostel)

Architect
Loughton Patterson

Resident/client profile
Ambulant, with highly challenging behaviours

DESCRIPTION OF BUILDING

Site context
Suburban

Number of resident beds
40

Number of respite or assessment beds
8

Details of other overnight accommodation
Motel-type guest unit

Kinross Hostel is situated opposite a local primary school.

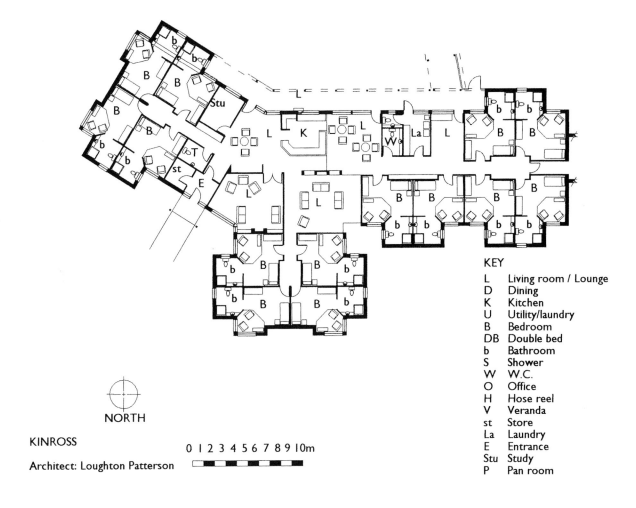

NORTH

KINROSS

Architect: Loughton Patterson

0 1 2 3 4 5 6 7 8 9 10m

KEY
L	Living room / Lounge
D	Dining
K	Kitchen
U	Utility/laundry
B	Bedroom
DB	Double bed
b	Bathroom
S	Shower
W	W.C.
O	Office
H	Hose reel
V	Veranda
st	Store
La	Laundry
E	Entrance
Stu	Study
P	Pan room

Plan form
Three houses (13, 13 and 14-units) securely linked.
A fourth house has eight respite units.

Communal and shared spaces for residents
Each house has a kitchen, dining room, family room, formal lounge and two communal toilets off each living area in each house. Activities room and chapel are centrally located.

Staff facilities
Staff room with kitchen facilities and outdoor area.

Office and administration space
Reception area and office for manager, plus supervisors' study in each house.

Service and ancillary spaces
Each house has own kitchen, separate laundry for personal clothes (linen is contract laundered). Each resident room has en suite facilities.

What site constraints or external factors such as existing buildings or local planning legislation, affected the form and planning of the building?
None.

Construction and external materials
Double brick and clay tile construction, powder-coated aluminium windows, paved covered walkways.

Type(s) of flooring
Bedrooms, lounges and passageways – carpet; kitchen and meals – timber parquet; bathrooms, WCs and laundries – ceramic tile.

Internal finishes
Ceilings – gypsum plasterboard, painted. Walls – generally plastered and painted, some timber panelling, wallpaper and face brick to identify areas.

Equipment
Hand rails and grab rails to bathrooms and toilets only

STAFFING

Management staff
Manager	0.5 FTE
Coordinator	1.0 FTE

Care staff
16 FTE direct care staff (including two "upright" staff at night)

Other staff
150 hours per week (clerk, domestics, gardener)

BUILDING STATISTICS

Site area
9,254m² (total site includes day centre and respite house).

Ground floor area i.e. "footprint"
2,120m²

Total floor area
2,120m²

Floor area of individual units of accommodation
23.5m² each (including en suite)

Design for Dementia

117

The main entrance. Kinross Hostel is part of a complex of dementia-specific facilities.

Floor area of common living and dining rooms per group or cluster as appropriate (excluding separate circulation space and corridors)
177m²

Building cost including fixed equipment, hard and soft landscaping (but excluding loose furniture and fittings and professional fees)
A$2.3 million

BUILDING DESIGN

The philosophy of care
Kinross Care Centre provides care for people who are ambulant and have dementia and related behaviour that precludes their needs being met appropriately in mainstream facilities.

Residents have behaviours such as determined wandering; trying to get to other places; sleep disturbances; nocturnal variation; disruptive, demanding behaviours such as agitation; severe disorientation; taking other people's belongings; disinhibited behaviour; repetitive sentences and mannerisms. They may be withdrawn; they may have difficulty in maintaining continence of urine and faeces. Residents need major assistance with personal hygiene; grooming and dressing. Many of the residents would otherwise be accommodated inappropriately in a nursing home setting.

It is Anglican Homes' philosophy that people with such needs have the right to a specialised environment, with properly trained and supported staff promoting their dignity and worth, enhancing their abilities and respecting their individuality. People without these needs living in mainstream hostels or nursing homes also have the right to a peaceful lifestyle which can be compromised by an integration model. Staff have the right to receive appropriate training (provided by Anglican Homes' Sir James McCusker Training Foundation),

adequate support of realistic staffing levels, financial inputs, chaplaincy and general corporate services. Also residents' relatives are made to feel welcome and involved. They have the right to know that their loved one is well cared for in an environment which does not label them as different, or their behaviour as embarrassing.

Well designed buildings will never substitute for well trained, caring staff in a supportive and appropriate management environment. Thus philosophy and objectives relate to issues other than buildings and conversely buildings must be complementary and supportive to other environments.

The hostel is part of a complex of dementia specific facilities – hostel, future separate respite cottage and day centre. In-home respite care is also intended for the future. Clients will then have a "one-stop shop" for dementia.

Siting
The centre is located adjacent to a small suburban shopping centre and opposite a primary and high school. Surrounding housing, all about five to six years old, is almost all single-storey new brick and tile.

External character and appearance
The external character and appearance gives the impression that the hostel is four large houses with individual street access, letter boxes and carports.

Approach and entrance
The approach and entrance is similar to surrounding housing.

Approach to signage and cueing
Relationships of bedrooms are well defined with all bedrooms leading to the living area. Cueing and wayfinding, and limiting choices are incorporated in floor plans, interior decorations and furniture.

Above, the front entrance. Below, residents have free access to the secure garden area .

Approach to colour schemes and interior design

Creating atmospheres of comfort and old fashioned welcoming with age-appropriate themes of furniture. Different themes are used for each house.

Security provisions

All the houses and grounds are fully fenced and secure, with sensor-activated security lighting. Access to the secure rear garden area is not restricted from within the house and residents can wander out at will. The kitchens overlook these gardens and give the staff excellent, unobtrusive oversight of the garden areas. Doors are key locked so that no relative can leave without seeing a staff member (therapeutic time).

Heating and/or ventilation system or air conditioning system

Heating: All living spaces have electric radiant ceiling heating, thermostatically and time clock controlled. Bathrooms have ceiling mounted light/heater combinations.
Cooling: All communal spaces have ducted evaporated cooling. Bedrooms have ceiling fans and offices and studies have reverse cycle air conditioning.

Technology used

Fire alarms and detection: Full smoke and thermal alarms, main fire indicator panel linked to the fire brigade via the telephone. The fire alarm is also linked to the pagers staff carry.

Emergency call and monitoring systems: A standard call system with radio pagers, but with no audible buzzers or flashing lights, has been used. This is supplemented by a monitoring system to assist night-time supervision and care.

Monitoring uses bed weight sensors and movement detectors. These are linked via computer software to programmable resident "profiles" in a data base. Only abnormal or unusual activity, which could indicate distress, will trigger an alarm on the emergency call system. The telephone system is also linked to pagers.

Success in meeting intentions

The completed building met all planned goals.

Major hurdles that had to be overcome or prevented the intentions from being achieved

Staff training in the monitoring system must be intensive and on-going.

Aspects of the building design worthy of replication?

Most features

To be avoided in the future?

Residents with dementia have difficulty negotiating sliding doors. Cleaning of floor tiles is difficult. Residents can get to the kitchen sink, so there is a risk of flooding.

Objectives	Strategies
PRIVACY & DIGNITY These are significant quality-of-life issues.	1. Treat residents with respect. 2. Carry out ablutions and dressing in private. 3. Reduce the perception of being locked in. 4. Allow for parting with visitors in a dignified manner.
TOO MANY PEOPLE There are often problems when too many residents are together.	1. Provide for small groups and retreat to private space.
INDEPENDENCE Many people perceive a loss of independence as the greatest drawback to life in a hostel.	1. Design the hostel and programmes so that resident activities are not necessarily dependent on others. 2. Maintain flexible programmes to encourage independence and choice.
ROUTINE How can we best establish a routine for each resident?	1. Minimise the number of staff to whom each resident relates.
FREEDOM OF MOVEMENT Containing residents' movements can induce stress. Where do we draw the line?	1. Allow maximum movement around the hostel. 2. Make restrictions discreet and non-threatening.
HOME Everybody wants a hostel like "home". What does "home" mean?	1. Make the environment as familiar as possible. 2. Allow for residents to have their own furniture, pictures, etc. in their private space. 3. Encourage feelings of belonging, security, pleasure.

Design for Dementia

Objectives	Strategies
OUTDOORS Many residents enjoy the outdoors.	1. Provide exciting outdoor spaces. 2. Allow for walking adjacent to the buildings. 3. Paths must all lead to somewhere – no dead-ends. 4. Verandahs for sitting out of sun and rain. 5. Provide stopping/rest points within garden. 6. Minimise views out of the site – to discourage wandering off site.
ANIMALS AND CHILDREN People relate well to animals and children – often they will not communicate with adults	1. The buildings and staff attitudes should encourage children to visit. 2. Provide attractive play equipment close to residents' outdoor spaces. 3. Develop visiting programmes with local schools. 4. Develop techniques for having animals on site: – pets where all residents in an area agree – visiting dog-clubs
ORIENTATION How easy can we make it for residents to find their way around?	1. Remove distractions eg. discreet access to non-accessible rooms. 2. Reduce the number of people that are together, and the size of the building. 3. Limit directional choices to two, where possible. 4. Build and decorate spaces to feel different from each other – use colour, light quality, spatial quality, furnishings, and details. 5. Minimise corridors, "dead-ends".
STAFF STRESS Problems and attitudes of staff clearly impact on residents. How can we reduce stress?	1. Provide comfortable, attractive retreats with TV kitchen and toilets. Not accessible by residents. Private outdoor space opening off retreat. 2. Minimise number of staff/resident relationships. 3. Ease the monitoring of residents: observability and technological monitoring.
ROLE OF STAFF The perception staff have of their role as carers must impact significantly on the residents.	1. Train to be resident-centred. 2. Give responsibility and accountability for total care (including freedom to do things their own way). 3. Management regime to encourage flexibility.
FLEXIBILITY It is difficult to design for a "typical" resident with dementia	1. Allow living spaces and resident personal spaces to be modified for changing uses and tastes. 2. Design communal spaces to be suitable for variety of purposes.
ACTIVITIES, SKILLS How should we best assess people's abilities? What sort of activities should we provide for?	1. Encourage a wide range of activities. 2. Allow for large scale activities (all the residents together) for: ● making friends; ● an outing; ● economics (events). 3. Make kitchens accessible to encourage familiar domestic activities. 4. Develop activities programme and staff resources.

Above, the activities room. Below, a resident's personal space.

The kitchen... the central focus of each house.

FEEDBACK FROM STAFF

Favourite places
The kitchen:
Central focus of each house. Why?

Staff are able to maintain a view of most of the house whilst in the kitchen, therefore they encounter residents as they wander by and are able to interact with them.

Meal preparations – residents become involved in this either through watching or participating, setting the tables, reminiscing and chatting.

Bedroom:
There are several choices of where to place furniture. The bed has a limitation of two to three positions due to the sensor/monitoring system. Staff report that the room is a good size to work in, each resident is able to furnish their room individually and the room is big enough for staff to assist the residents when needed. This is also a resident's private space where they receive visitors if they wish. The rooms are large enough for two armchairs.

Bathroom:
The sliding door leading into the bathroom has proven unsuccessful, residents tend to want to push the door rather than slide it. This is not only very frustrating for the resident but unsafe as the doors come off the rungs. The size of the bathroom enables two people (resident and carer) to move freely and easily in it.

Tiles – some of the choices of tiles, i.e. the unglazed ones prove very difficult to clean and unfortunately always look a bit "grubby" despite a huge effort from the domestic staff. Consequently these tiles will not be used again.

Activities
The central point of the Kinross Care Centre complex is the activities room. It provides a social meeting place in a "club house" type atmosphere. Many residents enjoy attending regularly and actively seek their way to the activity room. Due to the nature of the design, residents pass by the room throughout the day. This may be deliberate or by chance but they are all encouraged to drop in and stay a while.

The activity staff report that the room is used for relatives and visitors especially over the weekend. Often non-stop afternoon teas are served, children are encouraged and games are played. We have received lots of positive feedback from relatives regarding the weekend use of the activity room, it gives the resident the opportunity to "show off" their skills at craft or baking allowing them to do something for their visitors, this in turn promotes feedback, something to talk about and a sense of achievement.

The kitchen design within the activity room proved to be too small. Residents tended not to want to go into this area to help out, and the design was quite different from kitchens in the houses which the residents enjoyed. The activity kitchen has very recently been modified and enlarged. Staff now report that the residents are more drawn to this area, especially the long bench space where residents lean and chat or clear the tables, carrying the washing-up to the bench top. This was not possible before as there was no room.

The activity staff at times wish the room was a little larger to accommodate all the extra visitors.

Comments/Feedback

"Everyone's so kind – what a great job they do."

"It's always good to bring her back to this place."

"Staff are courteous, direct and professional at all times."

Staff recently received positive feedback when escorting a resident on an outside appointment: "You can tell this lady is well looked after by the way she is dressed, she looks lovely."

And a comment made by a consultant ontologist from a large hospital, regarding one of the residents, "I can see Mrs..... is well cared for as she is beautifully groomed, and I always notice these things."

"These surroundings are so welcoming and homely."

"The staff are so friendly and warm, it's not at all like a nursing home, more like a home."

"It's so good being able to bring the kids in when I visit, a lot of places don't like doing that."

"Dad has picked up so much since being here, his speech is clearer and I'm sure it's because he's encouraged to talk. He used to just lie on his bed in hospital as there was nothing to motivate him. It's just great seeing him like this."

EDITORS' COMMENTS
Kinross is a very new hostel for people with dementia in the rapidly expanding suburbs surrounding the city of Perth. The whole area is undergoing residential development and Kinross with its three houses is indistinguishable from the rest, Each house has a kitchen with a counter around it, at its heart. Off this are the sitting room, family room and dining room which are semi open-plan, providing alternative spaces which are nevertheless central to the bedroom areas in terms of the material used, carpets, mouldings, etc.

Like the Village at Inglewood, residents have somewhere to go during the day. The activities room and chapel are separate from the houses across the back yard. For many people going out of the home during the day will make a lot of sense.

The design of Kinross was based on the lessons learned by Anglican Homes from their first Lefroy specialist hostel for people with dementia which was the first in Australia. One of these lessons was the enormous distances walked by staff on each shift. Kinross remedies this with its smaller units and more compact layout.

The Meadows

Six reasons for selection

- Innovative service walkway • Facility plant and equipment removed from cottages.
- No dead ends • Good visual access • Monitoring system manages night-time safety and personal care by exception • Many different spaces for socialisation or privacy.
- Strong attention to detail. e.g. door handles, taps, picture rails

The Meadows
The Hammond Village
Thomas Avenue
Hammondville
NSW 2170
Australia
Tel: (+61) 2 9299 8222
Fax: (+61) 2 9299 3792

Owner
The Hammond Care Group

Contact person for further information
Rosemary Bond, Director of Care Services.
Tel: (+61) 2 9825 5010
Fax: (+61) 2 9825 1566

Type of building
40-bed dementia-specific residential hostel.

Architect:
Allen, Jack & Cottier
59 Buckingham Street
Surry Hills NSW 2010

Resident/client profile
Ambulant, with levels of confusion

DESCRIPTION OF BUILDING

Site context
Suburban, co-located on The Hammond Village site, which has three nursing homes with 150 residents and one other general hostel with 102 residents, self-care units and a day care facility in the suburb of Hammondville in the Greater Sydney region.

Number of resident beds
39

Number of respite or assessment beds
One

Details of other overnight accommodation
There are three parlours or lounge rooms which can be used by relatives or other guests to stay over, one per residence.

Plan form
There are three residential houses, two of which have 14 residents and one with 12 residents. The three houses are interconnected by an enclosed and discrete corridor which connects to the administration building. Each building has two short bedroom corridors that form a "Y" shape, with the foot being the activities areas of kitchen, living and dining rooms.

Communal and shared spaces for residents
The heart of each house is the kitchen, which opens onto a main living area, consisting of lounge and dining areas. There is an assisted toilet adjacent to this area. The front door and vestibule of each home for visitors and relatives opens onto this space.

There are three other internal communal spaces – a sunporch, a reading room and a parlour – and an external "summer house" or gazebo overlooking a pond. All of these areas provide "quiet" spaces to go to apart from the bedroom.

Staff facilities
There is a fourth "home" – the administration building – in which are located a staff room and kitchen, together with staff bathroom and lockers. Also included in this fourth building is a delivery and service space combined with storage rooms. This building is linked to each of the three resident homes by an internal walkway, providing unobtrusive access and egress from the rear of each homes' laundry and kitchen pantry. This allows services – laundry skips, trolleys and provisions – to be delivered unobtrusively and without disturbing the residents. It also provides secure round-the-clock access for staff, particularly at night. Maintenance of plant and equipment is also provided via this internal staff walkway.

Office and administration space
The administration building has, in addition to the service and delivery spaces and staff room and amenities, two offices and a reception area.

Service and ancillary spaces
Within the three residential cottages, all service and ancillary spaces are those found in ordinary domestic homes. There is one assisted bathroom, a domestic style laundry but no "institutional" spaces, such as sluice or pan rooms.

The covered way also accommodates non-domestic services. The re-stocking of pantries, the collection of dirty linen and supply of fresh linen, and the servicing of boiler units, air conditioning compressors, electricals and telephones all occur within this space external to the cottages.

What site constraints or external factors, such as existing buildings or local planning legislation, affected the form and planning of the building?
Need to utilise existing services; the need to relate to surrounding buildings; access provisions of existing roads; the site was relatively level; the buildings were oriented for optimum solar access and with the existing vegetation in mind; there was a need to keep the building above the flood plain.

Construction and external materials
Domestic type construction. Single-storey cavity brickwork on reinforced concrete slab, with tile-trussed framed roof.

Design for Dementia

Above, a jacaranda tree stands in front of a cottage entrance and front garden. Below, the view from a dining room and kitchen area. Note how hampers are used to visually shorten the corridor.

The kitchen is accessible to residents and used by them. There is a shutter and stable door for night security.

Type(s) of flooring
Carpet tiles throughout except all wet areas, kitchen and laundries which are seamless vinyl.

Internal finishes
Walls are painted cement render with timber wainscoting in hallways. Ceilings are painted plasterboard.

Equipment
Most equipment is domestic. In the en suite bathrooms, there are adjustable hand showers with extended hoses and night lights over the toilet; there is a central warm water system; and there are safety/grab rails.

STAFFING

Management staff
38 hrs/wk (manager)
Care staff
17 FTE (Full-Time Equivalents)
Other staff
80 hrs/wk

BUILDING STATISTICS

Site area within site boundaries
approx. 8,500m²

Ground floor area i.e. "footprint"
2,100m²

Total floor area
2,100m²

Floor area of individual units of accommodation,
16.8m² plus en suite bathroom of 4.3m²

Floor area of common living and dining rooms per group or cluster as appropriate (excluding separate circulation space and corridors)
Sitting and dining areas: 113.6m² in each of the three cottages, a total of 340.8m².
External paved areas (not including paths): 101m² per cottage, a total of 303m².

Building cost including fixed equipment, hard and soft landscaping (but excluding loose furniture and fittings and professional fees)
A$3.3 million

BUILDING DESIGN

The philosophy of care
The philosophy of care of the hostel is one that affirms the intrinsic value of each person and their right to respect and dignity. This philosophy seeks to promote quality of life through dignity, independence, safety, resident improvement and family participation and it is these principles by which The Meadows is measured.

It is recognised that the residents are elderly people with a particular illness, that of dementia. As such they are treated with the patience and courtesy normally extended to respected elders.

It is also considered important that the accommodation is appropriate for the resident and, for this reason, the principles of care are closely paralleled by resident admission and transfer criteria which enabled the architectural brief to cater for the

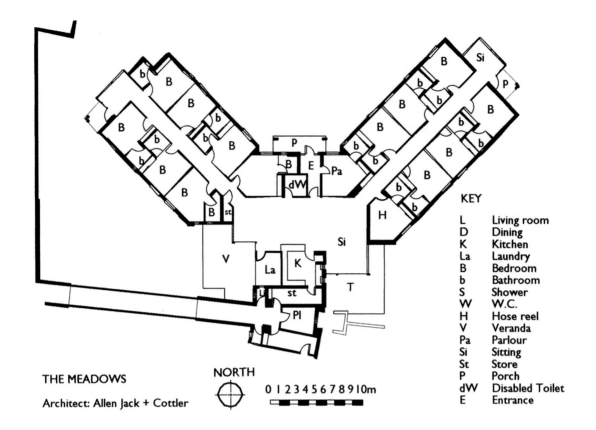

THE MEADOWS

Architect: Allen Jack + Cottler

NORTH

0 1 2 3 4 5 6 7 8 9 10m

KEY

L	Living room
D	Dining
K	Kitchen
La	Laundry
B	Bedroom
b	Bathroom
S	Shower
W	W.C.
H	Hose reel
V	Veranda
Pa	Parlour
Si	Sitting
St	Store
P	Porch
dW	Disabled Toilet
E	Entrance

least able resident, while at the same time having a picture of the "average" resident:

● The resident will be an older adult with diagnosis of Alzheimer's disease or other dementia.

● They will be mobile and require assistance with activities of daily living but be able to participate in domestic activities with guidance.

● The resident will be able to communicate their needs and be able to follow one-step directions.

● A person may be incontinent if it is manageable and some residents may require care for illnesses such as diabetes.

● The resident will not have a history of harm to self or others, have uncontrolled yelling or screaming behaviour, nor have a high risk of suicide or other psychiatric disorder.

In order to achieve this, the hostel has the following objectives:

● To provide a warm, domestic type of environment in which the person with dementia can feel at home, taking part in familiar activities.

● To provide the least restrictive environment necessary to ensure the security of wandering residents: any restrictions to wandering are kept as unobtrusive as possible. The option to secure the perimeter or other areas of the unit is available to the staff in times of need, e.g. at night or in the case of particularly restless residents.

● To assist residents to feel more secure and at home, the placement of old photographs or other treasured items in their own rooms is encouraged.

● To enhance self-esteem and well-being, the residents will be encouraged to do all they can for themselves and help each other and staff, even in minor ways, no matter how slowly it is done.

● To identify suitable clients through the process of assess-

ment and consultation with other health care services and agencies.

● To admit appropriate clients and formulate individual care and management plans through the process of observation, assessment and review, that is case management. These are to be completed within one month of admission and regularly updated.

● To work consistently with the residents through the implementation of individual care and management plans, maintaining and improving wherever possible their levels of independence and quality of life.

● To monitor and evaluate the effects of the care provided through on-going observation, assessment, management and review.

● To develop the skills of the staff and continue their education through the process of in-service lectures, discussions and case presentations, and also their attendance at relevant courses, workshops, conferences, etc.

● To support the families/friends of dementia sufferers both within the hostel and the community by links with day care and other support services for approved clients when time and other resources permit.

In short, the aim was to create a prosthetic environment which enables individuals to compensate for personal dysfunction.

Importantly, the building was only one part of that environment: it had to be a passive component of an integrated care system which focused upon "resident quality of life", "normalisation", and "person-centred resident care" rather than the more organisational and institutional issues of administration, supervision, maintenance, economy. In providing this compensation, the built environment would compensate for physical and intellectual deficits in an unobtrusive – almost imperceptible – manner.

How was the philosophy expressed in the design of the building?

Internally.

For residents:
- Visual access for residents.
- A domestic "homelike" environment rather than an institutional one.
- A minimum of distractions.
- A minimum of "through traffic".
- A minimum of extraneous noise.
- A secure environment (residents' perception).
- A central activities focus to the house, i.e. kitchen.
- Access to enclosed garden.
- A choice of areas that afford privacy or socialisation.
- Domestic – familiar – furnishings.
- Easy "wayfinding" for residents.
- Variety of sitting areas.
- Minimum of "dead-end" situations – and locked doors.
- Visibly obvious toilet facilities adjacent to bedrooms.
- Service delivery allowing security, consistency and routine, with minimal disruption for residents.

For relatives and friends.
- Overnight accommodation in each house.
- A variety of quiet sitting areas where they can be with residents, apart from bedrooms.
- All facilities, including the kitchen and laundry, where visitors can, "as normal", join in assisting with making tea, meals and other activities of daily living.

For staff:
- Secure access 24 hours for staff safety.
- Separate staff facilities in the administration house.
- Visual access works both ways allowing staff to see residents and all parts of building and external areas.
- Infra-red monitoring system for unobtrusive, non-interventionist provision of care allowing maximum privacy and independence for residents.
- The non-institutional environment emphasises to staff their personal care roles.

Externally

For residents:
From the street each house appears as a suburban home. This allows the individual the dignity of living "at home" with a separate street address and entrance; private back yard space with clothesline, barbecue, vegetable gardens and flower gardens, and an open front yard; walking spaces; and a summer house overlooking a pond.

For relatives and friends:
The Meadows is visitor-friendly. There are three backyards and three front yards providing both enclosed and open garden spaces where children can play safely and visitors can be entertained. Entrance is by a locked front door – just like one's own house.

The suburban home appearance ensures that relatives and friends have a positive perception of visiting a house rather than a large facility. Each of the three houses has its own street address and entrance and is designed with familiar detail and to an individual scale. Such a suburban environment supports community integration

For staff:
Secure access 24 hours for staff safety; parking spaces can be seen from central activity space

Plan form

"Y" plan form arranged to allow for maximum visual access to activity areas for staff i.e. from the kitchen, all sitting, dining, laundry, hallway and gardens are visible. As an aid to wayfinding there is maximum visual access to activity areas from hallway and vice versa.

There is interconnection between the cottages to address occupational health and safety issues, permit visual access and allow unobtrusive service delivery as well as allowing sustainable financial benefits.

External character and appearance

Familiar domestic/suburban character with pitched tiled roofs, gable ends, verandahs, face brickwork, double-hung windows, awnings, domestic garden beds and flowers and a non-institutional colour scheme.

Approach and entrance

Distinguished by pergola, letterbox and a garden path leading to a front door and porch.

Approach to signage and cueing

There is a minimum of signage – cueing is by association, e.g. cue frame photos and memorabilia at each bedroom.

Ensuring that there was as much visual access as possible at all times, coupled with the desire to ensure that all decisions made are the correct ones, meant that much signage and cueing was integrated into the building design rather than conspicuously layered on top of it. Potentially the most difficult situation to overcome was the problem of sameness existing when a resident is returning to their bedroom along a corridor. With a view to reducing actual or potential confusion caused by sameness, each individual's door would be decorated, or land-marked, with a collection of framed memorabilia. This personal frame would reinforce who the individual is and aspects of their life, thus validating their self-identity and worth and reinforcing their dignity.

Further, the design endeavoured to differentiate by using different light fittings, wall colours, diminishing the visual length of corridors by dividing them with hampers or screens and using different shaped and hence different feeling door handles to involve another sense in the process of recognition. The design endeavoured to facilitate the differentiation of decisions based on a common element, such as opening a door but differentiating between cupboard doors, entrance doors and toilet doors, by discerning use of colour or texture. Bedroom doors were not placed opposite one another so as not to invite a person leaving his/her room but unsure of their destination to simply proceed to the first room/door they see.

The residents' declining physical or intellectual abilities, including for some the ability to recognise danger, meant that a number of "aids" and safety strategies had to be incorporated. Thus taps are colour coded red and blue for hot and cold and are half-turn, easy grip style. Light and electrical switches are large plate rocker switches, and doors have lever action handles. Importantly, all these compensatory items are familiar to the long-term memory of the resident for they may not have the ability to learn new information and therefore unfamiliar items would not be utilised.

Approach to colour schemes and interior design

As indicated above, object rather than colour is used for cueing. The colour schemes are based on domestic colour combinations and were "high key" rather than "low key" (therefore with higher reflectants) in order to provide for the change in perception of colour with age. Each bedroom has a different "set" of colours. In addition, in the early twentieth-century Australians used brighter colour schemes.

Security provisions

Areas to which resident access may be limited for their safety were kept to a minimum. This was to reinforce personal mastery of the environment and to promote autonomy and dignity. To enable this, certain features were designed into the environment, e.g. windows have restricted openings, back yards are secure from the street.

It is worth noting that throughout two hundred years of European settlement, white Australians have felt "threatened" by the big open spaces and have feverishly fenced them. The end result is that culturally white Australians have felt anxious without a fence.

Above, view across dining area from living room towards back yard. Below, the back yard with path – note covered walkway – looks like a wall at the side of the garden.

Above, part of the living area at The Meadows. This lounge looks out onto the back yard. Below, the view from the gazebo on the edge of the pond showing circular walk from living rooms to the porch.

There are only two locked doors in each house: the front door and the service corridor to the pantries.

The issue of safety also involves poisons and electricity. Providing a locked cupboard in the laundry for detergents and small electrical items such as irons removed these hazards from resident access. Electricity and gas for the stove in the kitchen has remote switches for staff-only operation. The use of a locked drawer for sharp kitchen utensils and one locked cupboard for detergents means the kitchen is relatively safe for resident use. At night, when staffing levels are lower, the kitchen can be secured, if necessary, by a door and a shutter over the bench. The use of a "stable" door would allow a staff member to undertake kitchen tasks with elements of risk and "busy-ness", such as cutting/chopping or serving meals, without eliminating the residents' olfactory and visual access, and therefore their utilisation of the senses to stimulate memory.

Within every large building complex there would be items which pose risk to the uninformed and the unwary person, as well as a person experiencing physical and mental frailty. These include water, gas and electrical plants, and they are located so that both residents and the general public have no access to them. Access to these areas is limited to supervisory and maintenance teams to ensure staff safety by locating plant rooms at the internal junctions of the homes. Due to the design of the hostel, residents would have neither visual or physical access to these areas, which further reduces safety risks.

Heating and/or ventilation system or air conditioning system

The climate is temperate and there is natural ventilation of all areas. In addition there is split unit reverse cycle air-conditioning to main sitting and dining areas; central reticulated hot water to convection panels elsewhere.

Technology used

The Meadows employs an innovative resident monitoring system that is designed to maintain high standards of resident safety and carer awareness without impinging on the daily life or integrity of the resident.

The monitoring system achieves this by utilising a series of infra-red movement sensors networked to a computer monitoring program. This allows for each resident bedroom/en suite to be programmed to a particular set of resident behaviour patterns identified as "normal" for that resident.

Should there be a deviation from the previously assessed "normal" behaviour, e.g. incontinence, agitated movement, exiting of the bedroom, prolonged time in the en suite, etc., the computer will identify the problem and activate a vibrating pager alerting the carers on duty to the problem and its location. The pager system also allows for intercommunication between carers.

Success in meeting intentions

The intentions were achieved within the completed building.

Major hurdles that had to be overcome or prevented the intentions from being achieved

The major hurdles were set by ourselves to overcome the then-existing paradigm of design, which was that while small was best, it was economically unsustainable. The challenge was therefore to attain the feeling of smallness but be economically sustainable.

Another major hurdle was the regulatory authorities and their lack of understanding of the non-institutional character of this building as opposed to acute hospitals.

Aspects of the building design worthy of replication?

The application of the principle of visual access within a normal domestic environment, the integration of care programmes and building design, the use of technology which is consistent with the overriding philosophy of care as well as the attention to detail, such as cueing with different door handles, have been key features of The Meadows.

To be avoided in the future?

There are matters of detail: e.g.

- Double power points will not be used again, as they are confusing for residents.
- The pathway of one house from the street to the front door, while attractive, is inconvenient in wet weather and has a steeper gradient than the others.
- Wooden benchtops and kitchen cupboards have not worn well; will use a laminate.
- Domestic cooktops need to look domestic, but be constructed for heavier duty.
- In the future we will have vegetables as well as flowers in the garden.
- Currently there is carpet throughout: in the future we may lay a non-carpet surface in dining areas.
- There is currently limited space for servicing plant and equipment.

Feedback

There are resident meetings every three months in each cottage. In addition the Commonwealth Department of Health and Family Services' outcome standards monitoring team speaks with relatives and residents. All of the feedback to date has been extremely positive.

The daughter of one resident spoke at the 1996 Dementia Design Conference; two relatives were filmed on a video which was produced for the benefit of prospective residents and their relatives. All spoke positively of The Meadows. Two particular features mentioned frequently were the perception of safety and security; and the generous size of the bedrooms. There is also ongoing discussion with relatives with respect to the care plans (including medications if any) for the respective resident.

There are regular staff meetings and staff have had input into future developments of similar facilities, including those issues raised above.

EDITORS' COMMENT

The Meadows has applied the principle of total visual access – the capacity to sense or see where you are or want to go – in a different way from other examples in this book which have no corridors. A resident can see the communal areas from their bedroom door and, indeed, from anywhere in the cottage. In the bedrooms there is visual access to the en suite toilet from wherever the bed is placed. Conversely, personal care staff can see the entire cottage and its yards from the kitchen.

The challenge of reducing confusing decision-making without reducing choice and independence has been achieved by ensuring that choice remains, but that every choice is a right one. There are no dead ends and no matter which garden path is chosen the resident will return to the house and communal areas.

The principle of reducing extraneous stimuli and the institutional feel has been achieved by having the service walkway connecting the three cottages. This reduces the image of facility support, ensuring that linen and food services are delivered discreetly into the pantry and laundry of each cottage. Ensuring that all of the utilities and plant and equipment is removed from the cottages also means that the residents are not disturbed by unfamiliar faces.

The covered walkway also addresses occupational health and safety issues, enabling staff to walk safely between cottages at any time. The use of a computerised passive infra-red monitoring system, which manages "by exception", improves the safety and personal care programmes for residents while at the same using human resources effectively.

The Village

Reasons for selection

• *Strong relationship with surrounding 'Federation' streetscape* • *Good visual access with bedrooms integrated around living space* • *Clubhouse as an alternative place to visit* • *Extensive use of cueing both internally and externally* • *Attention to garden for therapeutic activity* • *Internal decor of communal areas: armchairs and lounges.*

The Village
Homes of Peace Inc
2 Walter Road
Inglewood 6052
Western Australia
Tel: (+61) 9 388 5300
Fax: (+61) 9 381 4559

Owner
Homes of Peace Inc.

Contact person for further information
Dr P. Flett, executive director or Mrs G. Peachment, consultant (facilities and planning) at Homes of Peace.

Type of building
Nursing home

Architect
Hobbs Winning Australia
37 Ord Street
West Perth 6005
Western Australia

Resident/client profile
Ambulant and non-ambulant with highly challenging behaviours

DESCRIPTION OF BUILDING

Site context
Suburban, integrated with an existing nursing home development and surrounding residential areas.

Number of resident beds
44

Number of respite or assessment beds
One day respite

Details of other overnight accommodation
None

Plan form
Two 10-bedroom houses. Three eight-bedroom houses and one clubhouse.

Communal and shared spaces for residents
Eight and 10-bed houses each have combined living and dining area, one lounge room, kitchen and laundry.
One fully assisted bathroom with Parker bath shared between two houses.

Staff facilities
Office space, staff WC, storeroom, cleaners' store, quiet room (in Clubhouse).

Office and administration space

10-bed house	6.57m² office space
8-bed house	9.10m² office space
Clubhouse	14.22m² office space

Service and ancillary spaces
Main kitchen on site plus kitchen in each house. Main laundry off site. Laundry for personal items in each house; this room also contains sanitiser and sluice. Separate dirty linen room, and clean linen storage.

What site constraints or external factors such as existing buildings or local planning legislation, affected the form and planning of the building?
Original ward demolished and The Village built on same site. The two-street frontage allowed scope to design imaginatively but existing site services (electricity, gas and sewerage) had to be accommodated.

Construction and external materials
Double brick and iron roof. Each house uses different coloured brick. Houses linked by covered walkways, secure on outer perimeter and open to grounds on inner courtyard, and landscaped gardens.

Type(s) of flooring
Living rooms: foyer and lounge carpeted with patterned wool plush pile carpet tiles. Bedroom: same but with bland pattern. Kitchens and laundries: vinyl. Bathrooms, staff toilets and en suites: Ceramic non-slip tiles in en suites. Clubhouse: wood tiles with wooden parquetry dance floor insert.

Internal finishes
Walls: painted plaster. No hand rails in large internal living room. Nine cofferdam ceilings, in this large room, four containing skylights.

Equipment
Two Parker baths in the whole complex. Each bedroom in each house has an en suite i.e. one shower, shower chair and fully assisted toilet to each bedroom. Sanitiser. (*See Service and ancillary spaces.*)

STAFFING

Management staff

Co-ordinator dementia services	20 hrs/wk
Clinical Nurse	38 hrs/wk
Care staff	
Registered nurses	203.5 hrs/wk

Design for Dementia

133

Above, each of the five units at The Village is individually named and has its own front door, entry lobby and convenient parking for guests. Below, specially designed paths allow residents to stroll as they like. Visual cues help them find their way back to their units — each of which has its own exterior colour and paving design.

Assistant nurse/carers   523.5hrs/wk
Enrolled nurses   269.5 hrs/wk
Other staff
Hotel Services   64 hrs/wk

BUILDING STATISTICS

Site area within site boundaries
Overall site area I approximately   7,900m²

Ground floor area i.e. "footprint"
2,315m²

Total floor area
As above. Accommodation is provided on a single floor.

Floor area of individual units of accommodation,
8-bed unit twin room with en suite   41.65m²
8-bed unit single room and en suite   31.209m²
10-bed unit twin room with en suite   42.84m²
10-bed unit single room and en suite   23.82m²

Floor area of common living and dining rooms per group or cluster as appropriate (excluding separate circulation space and corridors)
10-bed unit   137.4 m²
8 bed unit   99.25 m²
Clubhouse   81.85 m²
(lounge/activity area only – no corridors).

Building cost including fixed equipment, hard and soft landscaping (but excluding loose furniture and fittings and professional fees)
A$2,600,480

BUILDING DESIGN

The philosophy of care
The Village's Mission Statement is as follows:
The Dementia Unit team will work with family and significant others to meet the needs of the individual, through a multidisciplinary approach.

Residents will be supported by caring, committed staff who are specifically educated to promote a homelike environment and activities which maintain the individual's quality of life and optimise their independence.

This statement lives within the context of the Homes of Peace Mission Statement, which declares that the Homes aim "to enrich the lives of the elderly and younger people with disabilities, by providing specialised care services to assist them in achieving their desired quality of life".

The model of care in The Village is captured by the visual representation of a waterwheel *(Figure 1)*. This visual depiction of the waterwheel shows how the foundations support the large wheel. Radiating out from the hub are seven large paddles. The whole is driven by an elemental force, i.e. the residents and relatives.

This model was chosen as it conveyed the various aspects of the model of care in a dynamic, changing and interconnecting way. The pivotal point which is continuous in its motion and interconnects or directs action, is assessment. The concentric band around the hub denotes essential staffing issues. The paddles are listed below.

Behaviour
Refers to the resident and is individual. A problem-solving approach will be used to identify different behaviours as exhibited by the resident, to assess and define problems, set goals, look for reasons behind the behaviour/problem and develop strategies/interventions, with the aim of preventing, alleviating or minimising the problems and to evaluate the effectiveness of any intervention. To promote and facilitate positive behaviours, to enable residents to function in the house.

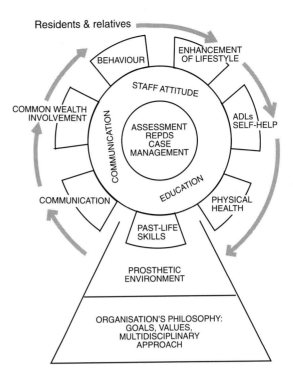

Figure 1. The 'waterwheel' model of care.

Activities of daily living (ADLs)
To ensure activities related to ADLs are as stress-free as possible, yet promoting and maintaining individual input into their ADLs. Skilled individual planning selects activities that can be successfully accomplished, at whatever level that may be.

Physical health
This care component includes physical fitness, balance, co-ordination, overall physiological status, pain management and the re-establishment or maintenance of function.

Past life skills
Each resident's previous roles, interests, hobbies and cultural background will be assessed and activities planned to enhance/maintain the individual's feeling of self-worth and identity within the person's day-to-day life. Again, we plan for individual success and accomplishment.

Communication
Identification and assessment of the resident's way of communicating with others. To develop strategies/interventions to enhance/maintain their ability to communicate with others within their environment or to develop alternative forms of communication.

Community involvement
Identification and assessment of the resident's previous involvement/interests in the community with the aim of maintaining those links for as long as possible through visits and outings. If necessary finding alternative ways of maintaining those links through visits from individuals or community groups to the resident in the unit. The Clubhouse provides a very flexible and accommodating facility for this purpose.

Enhancement of lifestyle
Identification of what makes life meaningful for the individual. This may have been touched on within the other aspects of care, i.e. past life skills, community involvement, etc.

It is envisaged that residents living in a purpose-built dementia unit with staff skilled in dementia care and with a positive attitude to their care will create an environment which is as stress-free for the individual resident as possible.

This reduction in stress and identification of what is meaningful for the individual may well lessen the occurrence of disordered behaviour.

Design for Dementia

135

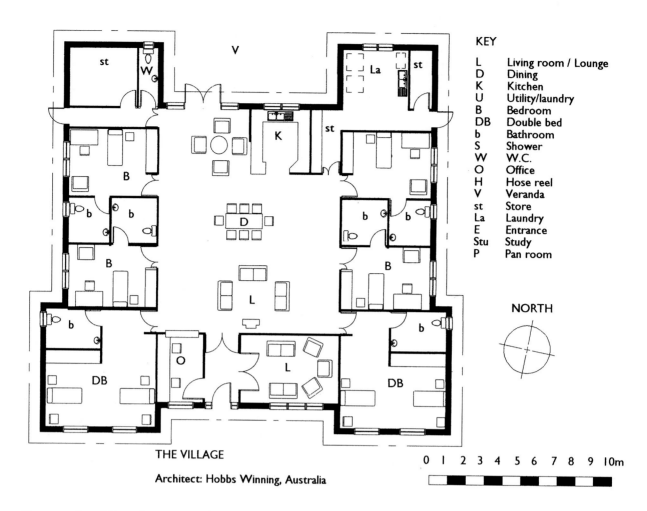

KEY

L	Living room / Lounge
D	Dining
K	Kitchen
U	Utility/laundry
B	Bedroom
DB	Double bed
b	Bathroom
S	Shower
W	W.C.
O	Office
H	Hose reel
V	Veranda
st	Store
La	Laundry
E	Entrance
Stu	Study
P	Pan room

NORTH

THE VILLAGE

Architect: Hobbs Winning, Australia

0 1 2 3 4 5 6 7 8 9 10m

How was the philosophy expressed in the design of the building?

Internally. For residents: To reduce confusion by eliminating dead ends, corridors and conflicting methods. To assist decision-making by making a small range of choices accompanied by total visual access.

To create an environment which is familiar, to assist recognition of the function of each room and a person's role within this space. To offer sensory support to lessen the impact of cognitive impairment. To capitalise on the sensory modalities, e.g. sound – reduction of noise levels; touch – offering a range of tactile experiences; sight – an uncluttered environment which gives visual stimulation and pleasure; taste/smell – accessible kitchen and related activities. All of these relate to both the behaviour paddle and the past life skills.

ADLs and self-help are supported through design by having individual en suites, where toilets are visible from the bed, and hand-held shower extensions allow residents to sit while showering.

Physical health is promoted by reducing anxiety with the built environment, creating the opportunity for choices without agitation, thus promoting self-confidence, which in turn promotes the value of the individual. All of this contributes to enabling a person to maintain function for as long as possible.

Although enhancement of lifestyle and community involvement occur within each house, the Clubhouse optimises this approach to care. The Clubhouse offers multiple opportunities for life enhancement. It is somewhere for people to go, to work, to a concert, for physical activities, to a dance, for a family reunion, for a sing along, yet also a place for a quiet sit, a church service, a meeting house. These activities are supported by friends, relatives and carefully selected community helpers.

Relatives and friends: Design for people with dementia is based on the needs of people and of the community. Design

needs are the same – comfort, a pleasant sensory input, dignity, privacy, choices. The design of The Village therefore supports both residents and relatives.

Externally

The sweeping grounds at the rear of the houses have been landscaped with paths suitable for wanderers and pacers. Extensive walking is possible without coming to a stop. Paths lead to each house and the Clubhouse through gardens offering visual (seasonal) and olfactory variety. A car offers reminiscence (sitting in it) or the opportunity for past life skills, washing and polishing. Each house has visible cueing devices for wayfinding.

Siting and plan form

The development is a complex situated at the north of an existing site; five houses are arranged in a semi-circle with the Clubhouse as an internal central focal point or hub. Residential frontage to two main streets integrates The Village with surrounding residential housing. Each Village house has access to a central garden area. The total development is enclosed and secure in an unobtrusive way.

External character and appearance

The development presents five individual houses built in a federation style to complement the existing suburban residential style.

Approach and entrance

The houses all have their own front doors, with parking facilities adjacent to each house for visitors.

Approach to signage and cueing

Signage is kept to a minimum. The name of each house is traditionally presented on a board mounted by the entrance. All residents are assessed for reading ability. Only those who can recognise their name have this placed on their bedroom door. Cueing is used far more extensively. Houses each have an external motif and this is presented in primary colours on a large plaque wall-mounted near the glass external doors. Matching transparencies are used on the glass doors. This reinforces the uniqueness of the motif to each house.

Approach to colour schemes and interior design

The average age is 85, and people of this longevity very frequently have visual impairment from a variety of causes. Pale colours cannot be seen and must be used in contrast if they are to have any effect.

Colour is used extensively. This is based on two factors. Firstly the aim is to be seen. Colour needs to be used strategically so that perception of space is not disrupted. Secondly colour is used to create a sensory enlivening environment. Individuals adjust to one colour very quickly, and the colour is "not seen". Variety reduces this action.

Interior design was based on the concept of creating an environment which did not seek to recreate the past specifically; instead we sought an ambience which suggested familiarity and comfort. This assists the delivery of care through facilitating reminiscence and sensory stimulation.

Furniture, artworks, lighting, flooring were all selected with this in mind. Seating was studied in depth. Appropriate seating was selected to reduce agitated behaviour, support function, assist socialisation and to offer tactile surfaces of great variety.

Security provisions

"Duress" call pendants are worn by night staff, interfaced with nurse call systems. The front doors are magnetically locked and require a code to exit. External fence gates are mechanically locked with coded locks. All bedroom doors have monitoring devices for silent hours operation.

Heating and/or ventilation system or air conditioning system

Radiant ceiling foil heating throughout, remotely controlled and monitored. Imitation (gas-fired) log fires in each lounge. Ducted evaporated air-conditioning to living areas, ceiling sweep fans in bedrooms.

Technology used

Door monitoring, cueing lights above WC pedestals, enhanced communications throughout extended facilities being available via the nurse call system.

Success in meeting intentions

Basically we achieved what we set out to do. With more experience some things would be altered, but our 1995 concept was attained.

Major hurdles that had to be overcome or prevented the intentions from being achieved

In this development, we were very fortunate to be able to build a completely new facility to our own design. The current hurdles are concerned with funding, rather than building or design.

Although the funding issue is a governmental issue, and not within our control, it has very relevant impact on staffing levels. The design of the building depends on certain staffing levels. If these levels are less a different design with much closer links between houses, would be the only financially viable option.

Aspects of the building design worthy of replication?

The integrated concept, i.e. bedrooms (with their own en suites) around the living space; no corridors, good visual access. The Clubhouse, detached and set apart, yet the focus of the garden area. The landscaping, offering seasonal plantings, different colours associated with each house, and well planned pathways and sitting spots.

To be avoided in the future?

Our service delivery needs to be improved. There was not enough recognition of its impact during planning. Service access is difficult, in that food and linen are brought in along pathways that are designed for residents; not efficient service delivery.

The living areas are probably a little large and the two double bedrooms do not offer the advantage we had anticipated, single bedrooms are better.

Feedback

Residents: Direct feedback not possible because of level of dementia. However in every case where a person comes with behavioural problems (aggressive, intrusive, verbal disruption, wandering to escape), this has settled. Enjoyment in Clubhouse activities is patently obvious, people finding their own way there.

Friends and relatives: Two successive customer satisfaction-surveys indicate a high level of satisfaction from the respondents in the care and other services.

Some families participated in The Village management unit, and those who wish, are involved in planning resident's care. They feel free to come and go, and join in, as they please. There are no barriers.

Families indicate that here their loved one feels like a "normal" person, not "different" as in other nursing homes. The freedom to roam around and join in "normal" activities, in a "normal" setting, is what sets this unit apart.

Staff: Some staff state they could not work in a traditional setting again saying that the design "does a lot of their work" for them. Valued points are the visual access within each house and over the garden; the design minimises confusion for residents; and the Clubhouse forms a real focus, for "going out" and "coming home" every day.

EDITORS' COMMENT

From the street, The Village looks much like other early twentieth-century homes in Perth, Western Australia. The brickwork, gables and exterior detail resonate with typical "Federation" houses.

The key design feature of The Village is the visual access available within each cottage. The bedrooms are integrated around the living space. There are no corridors from the bedrooms to the living areas: all of the bedrooms open immediately onto the living and dining and kitchen areas.

The situation of the Clubhouse as the focus of the garden area is another feature of The Village. It is detached from the homes and yet readily accessible, providing a special place to go each day, complete with dance floor, piano and club-style tables and chairs.

As well as the passive cueing provided by the visual access of the cottage's design, The Village has employed multiple cues where possible: the bedroom doors have different panelling and colours, the sliding doors leading to the gardens are decorated with decals in the style of stained glass to ensure that residents recognise closed doors; while, in order to assist residents' "wayfinding" from the gardens to their own house, there are individual icons for each house.

Above, there are no corridors at The Village, but wide spaces and circulation areas enable residents to see their overall living space from anywhere in their unit. Below, the kitchen area has a simple layout with an open view of the living room and bedrooms.

Above and below, the Clubhouse is a unique and highly successful feature of The Village, providing a special place to go each day. A kitchen in the Clubhouse means that the area is self-contained and can be used for small or large functions for residents and their families.

Les Parentèles

- Similar in scale and style to adjoining buildings • Generous space standards
- Compact, repetitive three-storey plan
- Tiled floor and other finishes typical of French apartments.

Name and address of building
Les Parentèles
4 rue de l'Hotel Dieu
95750 Chars
France
Tel: 01 34 32 80 00

Owner
Les Parentèles, 78219 Maurepas

Contact person for further information
Dr Georges Patat, General Manager

Type of building
Residential home

Architect:
M. Jean François Nicol
16 rue de la République
95570 Bouffemont
France

Resident/Client Profile
Ambulant and non-ambulant with highly challenging behaviours. Ambulant, with levels of confusion

DESCRIPTION OF BUILDING

Site context
Edge of village

Number of resident beds
60

Number of respite/assessment beds or other overnight accommodation
Six (respite or guest)

Plan form
Six groups of ten residents.

Communal and shared spaces for residents
Kitchen, sitting room/lounge, activities room.

Staff facilities
Large staff room with kitchen. Overnight room with en suite shower.

Office and administration space
Director's office. Two other office spaces.

Service and ancillary spaces
Main kitchen, laundry (residents' clothes and bed linen is outsourced). Linen stores (one per cluster). One infirmary per cluster (for emergencies).

What site constraints or external factors, such as existing buildings or local planning legislation, affected the form and planning of the building?
None known. The three-storey building fits well into the existing village environment.

Construction and external materials
Brick or concrete block with concrete floors and rendered externally.

Type(s) of flooring
Tiled floor throughout.

Internal finishes
Smooth plaster, fine textured render. Demountable ceilings to circulation spaces.

Equipment
Large assisted shower room.

STAFFING

Management staff
Part-time therapist and doctor of medicine and gerontology
Care staff
Two nurses, nine core staff (seven day, two night)
Other staff
16 domestic staff (14 day, 2 night)
NB: Two staff teams alternate on a two-week cycle.

BUILDING STATISTICS

Site area within site boundaries
410m²

Ground floor area i.e. "footprint"
1,000m²

Total floor area
3,000m²

Floor area of individual units of accommodation
23m²

Floor area of common living and dining rooms per group or cluster as appropriate (excluding separate circulation space and corridors)
88m²

Building cost including fixed equipment, hard and soft landscaping (but excluding loose furniture and fittings and professional fees)
17 million francs.

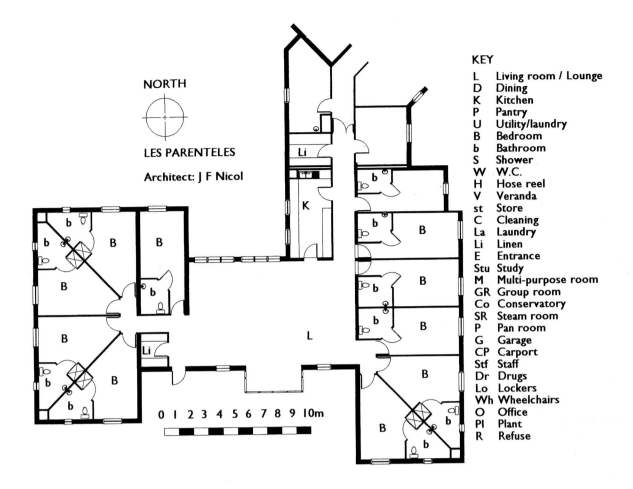

NORTH

LES PARENTELES

Architect: J F Nicol

0 1 2 3 4 5 6 7 8 9 10m

KEY

L	Living room / Lounge
D	Dining
K	Kitchen
P	Pantry
U	Utility/laundry
B	Bedroom
b	Bathroom
S	Shower
W	W.C.
H	Hose reel
V	Veranda
st	Store
C	Cleaning
La	Laundry
Li	Linen
E	Entrance
Stu	Study
M	Multi-purpose room
GR	Group room
Co	Conservatory
SR	Steam room
P	Pan room
G	Garage
CP	Carport
Stf	Staff
Dr	Drugs
Lo	Lockers
Wh	Wheelchairs
O	Office
Pl	Plant
R	Refuse

BUILDING DESIGN

The philosophy of care
To give a feeling of security to the residents and enhance their quality of life.

How was the philosophy expressed in the design of the building?
An overnight room and access to the kitchens has been provided for the benefit of residents and their relatives. For staff, good surveillance and visibility has been provided and there is easy evacuation of the building in an emergency.

Externally there is a secure door with interphone access. Easy parking facilities are provided.

Siting
The building's two wings open onto the garden on the north, which is closed to the south along the access road. The building respects the proportions of adjoining buildings.

Plan form
Central core and two wings, one on either side of core set at 45 degrees.

External character and appearance
Fits in well with the village vernacular in spite of its size.

Approach and entrance
Sets building slightly apart from the rest of the village.

Approach to signage and cuing
Small "dymo-type" signs on doors. Residents' rooms with small name labels, each a different colour, in top corner.

Approach to colour schemes and interior design
Warm colours have been used.

Security provisions
Everything is kept locked away. A key is required to enter the home and a keypad is used to get out.

Heating and/or ventilation system or air conditioning system
Radiators, combined with natural ventilation throughout, reduce the need to open doors and windows. Windows are double glazed.

Technology used
Doors and windows can be opened from a central control point in each wing.

Aspects of the building design to be avoided in the future?
Better distribution of meeting and activities rooms could have been provided.

Feedback
The staff have commented that the planning of the buildings assists staff in carrying out their work.

EDITORS' COMMENTS
Les Parentèles is a large three-storey building on the outskirts of Chars, an unassuming village set in rolling countryside north west of Paris. In spite of its size it relates well to an adjoining residential development and barely reveals its function from the approach road.

It houses 60 residents in six clusters of 10. The plan form is of two dumb-bell shaped clusters each of 10 individual bedrooms directly adjoining a living and dining room joined by central core of shared facilities to create a building which relates well to the entrance road and encloses sheltered garden spaces to the rear. The ambience is of a scheme of distinctive apartments, or perhaps a hotel.

Design for Dementia

Above, Les Parentèles, showing the village of Chars beyond. Below, the building's exterior showing balconies, french windows, roller shutters and bay windows.

Design for Dementia

Above, a bay window in the living/dining room. Below, the dining room – note the generous floor areas.

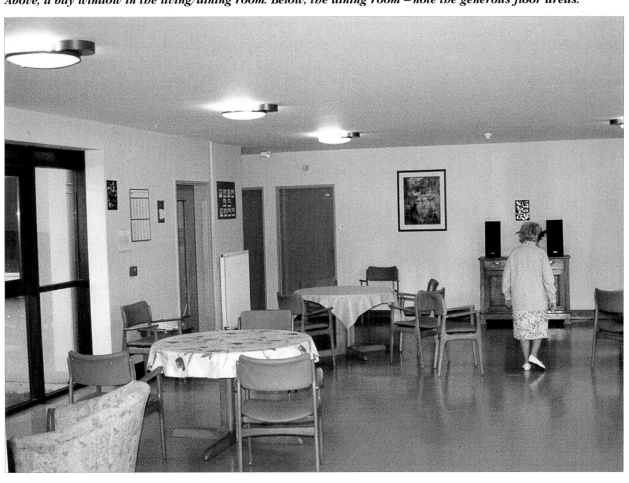

One immediately striking feature is the generous space standards The living/dining rooms provide 8.8m² per resident, between 4m² and 5m² is nearer the average for European examples, but the plan arrangement does keep circulation space to a minimum and provide good visual access from the doors into all bedrooms. It allows space for therapy activities to take place, visitors to sit with their relatives, all without interfering with other residents.

Bedroom sizes are also generous varying from 21m² to 23m² per single room including en suite shower. There are two bedroom types, one of which is triangular, which may help residents recognise their own rooms.

A well-equipped kitchen in one of the clusters at Les Parentèles.

Ancillary spaces are also generous, including a room for overnight use by relatives, a medical room and general purpose room used as an office for counselling relatives, or as a quiet room, in each cluster. There is also office accommodation and a central kitchen.

The generous space standards and floor to ceiling heights with the preponderance of hard, tiled floor finishes throughout give the building a very French character which is at variance to that which Australians, British and perhaps Scandinavians, think of as "homely". It is a reminder that France is a Mediterranean country as these characteristics are very typical of buildings of that region and it does influence the character of all French building, including modest apartment blocks.

The kitchen is a separate room and resident visitors do not appear to be encouraged. There is no personalisation of individual rooms or other spaces, no attempt to make individual rooms or doors recognisable. The care regime is handed down rather than participatory but the informality and "user-friendly" approach of the care staff makes Les Parentèles unique.

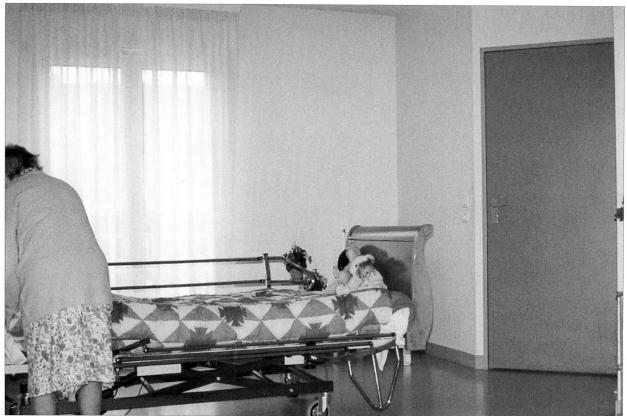

Typical room with en suite shower to the right.

Bibliography

Aldersgate Village – An Experiment in the Design of a Client Centred Nursing Home in Architecture Australia, Vol. 76, No. 3, May 1987, Pages 91-94.

Calkins M P (1988) *Design for Dementia Planning: Environments for the Elderly and the Confused* Maryland: National Health Publishing.

Cohen U and Day K (1993) *Contemporary Environments for People with Dementia*. Maryland: The Johns Hopkins University Press.

Cohen U and Weisman G D (1991) *Holding on to Home: Designing environments for people with dementia* Maryland: The Johns Hopkins University Press.

Hostel Design Guidelines Prepared for the Department of Community Services, Canberra, 1988.

Coons D H (1991) *Specialised Dementia Units.* Baltimore and London: The Johns Hopkins University Press.

Fleming R and Bowles I (1987) *Units for the Confused and Disturbed Elderly: Development, Design, Programming and Evaluation.* Australian Journal on Ageing 6, 4, 25-28.

Hiatt L G (1995) *Understanding the Physical Environment.* Pride Institute Journal of Long Term Care 4(2)12-22.

Kidd B J & Kidd L A *The Image of Home: Alternative Design for Nursing Homes* Research Discussion Paper, Centre for Applied Research on the Future, University of Melbourne, November 1987.

Kitwood T and Benson S (Eds) (1995) *The New Culture of Dementia Care.* London: Hawker Publications.

Lawton M P (1987) *Strategies in Planning Environments for the Elderly* Journal of Independent Living.

Lindesay J, Briggs K, Lawes M, Macdonald A, and Herzberg I (1991) *The Domus Philosophy: a Comparative Evaluation of a New Approach to Residential Care for the Demented Elderly* International Journal of Geriatric Psychiatry 6(10), 727-736.

Murphy E (1986) *Dementia and Mental Illness in the Old.* London: Papermac.

Netten A (1993) *A Positive Environment.* Aldershot: Ashgate Publishing.

Norman A (1987) *Severe Dementia: The Provision of Long Stay Care.* London: Centre for Policy on Ageing.

Peppard N R (1991) *Special Needs Dementia Units: Design, Development and Operations.* New York: Springer Publishing Company.

Plaisier A J, Douma A T, Fahrenfort M, Leene G J F (1992) *Het Anton Pieckhofje: Een woon-zorg-voorziening voor dementerende oudern, Evaluatie van een experiment (The Anton Pieckhofje: a domestic 'warm-care' service for old people with dementia. The evaluation of an experiment).* Nationaal Zieckenhuis Instituut: Utrecht and Vrije Universiteit: Amsterdam.

Ritchie K, Colvez A, Ankri J, Ledesert B, Gardent H, Fontaine A (1992) *The Evaluation of long-term care for the dementing elderly: a comparative study of hospital and collective non-medical care in France.* International Journal of Geriatric Psychiatry 7, 549-557.

Shroyer J L, Hutton J T, Gentry M A, Dobbs M N and Ehas J W (1989) *Alzheimer's Disease: Strategies for Designing Interiors:* The ASID Report Vol XV (2) June-July 1989.

Taira E D (1990) *Adaptations of the physical environment to compensate for sensory changes* In Ageing in the Designed Environment, New York and London: The Haworth Press, pp5.

Valins M (1988) *Housing for Elderly People: A guide for architects and clients.* London: Architectural Press.

Wilkinson TJ, Henschke PJ and Handscombe K (1995) *How should Toilets be Labelled for People with Dementia?* Australian Journal on Ageing 13 (4), 163-165.

Index

Design for Dementia